A QUIET EVOLUTION

The Emergence of Indigenous–Local Intergovernmental Partnerships in Canada

Much of the coverage surrounding the relationship between Indigenous communities and the Crown in Canada has focused on the federal, provincial, and territorial governments. Yet it is at the local level where some of the most important and significant partnerships are being made between Indigenous and non-Indigenous peoples.

In *A Quiet Evolution*, Christopher Alcantara and Jen Nelles look closely at hundreds of agreements from across Canada and at four case studies drawn from Ontario, Quebec, and Yukon Territory to explore relationships between Indigenous and local governments. By analysing the various ways in which they work together, the authors provide an original, transferable framework for studying any type of intergovernmental partnership at the local level. Timely and accessible, *A Quiet Evolution* is a call to politicians, policymakers, and citizens alike to encourage Indigenous and local governments to work towards mutually beneficial partnerships.

CHRISTOPHER ALCANTARA is an associate professor in the Department of Political Science at Western University.

JEN NELLES is a visiting associate professor in the Department of Urban Affairs and Planning at Hunter College.

D1508887

The Institute of Public Administration of Canada Series
in Public Management and Governance

Editors:

Peter Aucoin, 2001–2
Donald Savoie, 2003–7
Luc Bernier, 2007–9
Patrice Dutil, 2010–

This series is sponsored by the Institute of Public Administration of
Canada as part of its commitment to encourage research on issues in
Canadian public administration, public sector management, and public
policy. It also seeks to foster wider knowledge and understanding among
practitioners, academics, and the general public.

For a list of books published in the series, see page 161.

A Quiet Evolution

The Emergence of Indigenous–Local Intergovernmental Partnerships in Canada

CHRISTOPHER ALCANTARA
AND JEN NELLES

IPAC
The Institute of
Public Administration of Canada

IAPC
L'Institut d'administration
publique du Canada

UNIVERSITY OF TORONTO PRESS
Toronto Buffalo London

© University of Toronto Press 2016
Toronto Buffalo London
www.utorontopress.com
Printed in the U.S.A.

Reprinted in paperback 2017

ISBN 978-1-4426-3114-4 (cloth)   ISBN 978-1-4875-2264-3 (paper)

♾ Printed on acid-free, 100% post-consumer recycled paper.

Library and Archives Canada Cataloguing in Publication

Alcantara, Christopher, 1978–, author
A quiet evolution : the emergence of indigenous–local intergovernmental
partnerships in Canada / Christopher Alcantara and Jen Nelles.

(Institute of Public Administration of Canada series in public management
and governance)
Includes bibliographical references and index.
ISBN 978-1-4426-3114-4 (cloth).   ISBN 978-1-4875-2264-3 (paper)

1. Native peoples – Canada – Politics and government – Case studies.
2. Native peoples – Canada – Government relations – Case studies.
3. Local government – Canada – Case studies.   4. Regionalism –
Canada – Case studies.   I. Nelles, Jen, 1979–, author.   II. Institute of
Public Administration of Canada, sponsoring body.   III. Title.
IV. Series: Institute of Public Administration of Canada series in public
management and governance.

E92.A43 2016   320.8089'97   C2016-902510-1

University of Toronto Press acknowledges the financial assistance to its
publishing program of the Canada Council for the Arts and the Ontario
Arts Council, an agency of the Government of Ontario.

 Canada Council Conseil des Arts
for the Arts du Canada

ONTARIO ARTS COUNCIL
CONSEIL DES ARTS DE L'ONTARIO
an Ontario government agency
un organisme du gouvernement de l'Ontario

Funded by the   Financé par le
Government   gouvernement
of Canada   du Canada

 Canadä

For Kerry Lee Hunt-Alcantara, Kees Alcantara, Adelaide Alcantara, and Anthony Alcantara

For Robby Gutmann

Contents

Figures and Tables

Figures

Tables

Foreword

Canadians can easily be forgiven for thinking that relations between governments and the peoples of the First Nations are really an affair of the federal government. This is certainly true of the critically important aspect of funding, and scholars have devoted many hours to studying that relationship and recommending reforms that could improve that often tense relationship. But there are many other aspects to the intergovernmental relations of Aboriginal bands, and this book focuses on the much less understood dimension of local interactions.

I use the word "interactions" with particular purpose because the rapport between natural neighbours has not always been harmonious and sometimes has actually defied the very notion of "relations." All the same, there are many very successful cases across the land where Indigenous governments and cities, towns, and villages do collaborate, but we are still at a stage, it has to be said, where mistrust reigns.

The thinking on this subject has evolved. Twenty years ago, the Department of Indian Affairs and Northern Development, the Federation of Canadian Municipalities, and the Indian Taxation Advisory Board launched a Centre for Excellence in Municipal–Aboriginal Relations. Its mission was "to promote effective municipal–Aboriginal relations based on the principles of mutual recognition, respect, sharing, and mutual responsibility," and it set out to document actual agreements and practices. Out of that emerged a Centre for Municipal–Aboriginal Relations (CMAR) in 2001 to focus on solutions. It spawned a Municipal–Aboriginal Adjacent Community Cooperation Project committee to conduct further research, and it identified a number of splendid examples of collaboration in many parts of the country.

A small program was then put together in 2011 by the Federation of Canadian Municipalities and the Department of Aboriginal Affairs and Northern Development Canada called the First Nations–Municipal Community Infrastructure Partnership Program (CIPP). The program's mission was not to provide funding, but instead to offer tools and resources to facilitate the interchange between the communities. The ambition was that these resources would, in turn, lead to time- and money-saving partnerships focused on infrastructure. The program targeted "hard services" such as potable water provision, fire protection, landfill usage, and both wastewater and solid waste collection. It also included "soft services" such as policing, inspections, parks and community building maintenance, and even libraries.

The program was designed because there was a recognition that the communities where collaboration was acutely needed were typically small, and often very remote. There was also a recognition that relationships had been strained and that political differences were sometimes a real obstacle. The program has offered new approaches where needed, particularly where there was a lack of capacity on both sides to address urgent issues. The program has been a success, with more than thirty agreements signed and hundreds of workshops held across the country. It was recently one of the winners of the Institute of Public Administration of Canada–Deloitte Leadership Award.

The CIPP directors recognize that there are real issues that need to be overcome. Legislative challenges often make collaboration difficult as some questions fall under provincially controlled municipal acts and others fall under federal law. Priorities are often modified as a result of political changes, or because communities on either side do not have the capacity to imagine, negotiate, and then deal with the inevitable irritants that come out of any arrangements. Challenges aside, there is ample room to be optimistic that local collaboration can indeed be a key to better, faster development.

In this welcomed book, Christopher Alcantara and Jen Nelles probe a promising area of policy. Using deeply researched case studies, they project a new theory of what it takes to make these arrangements work. Better still, they give indications as to how mere arrangements can actually blossom into mutually reinforcing partnerships. It is an auspicious route that is eminently deserving of attention.

The Institute of Public Administration of Canada sponsors this series to shed light on new theories, new understandings, and new knowledge. I find great reward when researchers dig their spades at the intersection of different lines of inquiry. In this case, municipal management and the management of Indigenous communities come to life. The research is innovative and rich with insight, and it yields a useful framework. It fits perfectly with the mission of the series to support books on municipal affairs, and it also points the way to the future. There is a whole world of Aboriginal public management that needs to be explored, documented, and understood. In this field, this book is an important milestone.

Patrice Dutil, PhD
Ryerson University
Editor, IPAC Series in Public Management and Governance

Acknowledgments

This book came about almost by happenstance. We first met as part of the cohort of PhD students who had entered the University of Toronto's political science program in 2003 – a cohort that included a number of "superstars" such as Chris Cochrane, Glen Coulthard, Vincent Pouliot, and some others who are now working as associate professors across Canada (I think it is safe to say that we both flew under the radar!). In 2007, both of us were putting the finishing touches on our first major research projects as professional academics – Jen on inter-municipal cooperation in Germany and Canada, and Chris on comprehensive land claims negotiations in Labrador and Yukon Territory, Canada. Although we had long known about each other's research projects in general terms, we didn't realize how close our topics and interests were until one of us presented our research formally to the other (it may have been when Chris presented his mock job talk to the department prior to interviewing at Concordia University and Wilfrid Laurier University). One thing led to another, and we ended up publishing what we thought would be a one-off in the *Canadian Journal of Political Science* on First Nation–municipal cooperation in modern treaty negotiations.

In 2008 and fresh out of grad school, we decided to apply for a SSHRC Standard Research Grant to do a major study of Indigenous–municipal intergovernmental relations in Canada but we were unsuccessful. The next year, we decided to resubmit the same application with only minor revisions in response to comments from the previous competition, and again it was rejected. Finally, in 2010, we again submitted the application, this time completely unchanged, and it was funded! And so the hard work began. Given that this was our first major (and solo!) research project as newly minted PhDs, there was a steep learning curve

at first. The fact that you are reading this book now is a testament to
the many people and organizations that supported our work and this
project since 2008.

From a financial standpoint, this project was made possible by a
SSHRC Standard Research Grant. More recently, the final stages of our
project have been supported by an Ontario Early Researcher Award,
which we are using to expand our study to include relationships in
New Zealand and the United States. We thank both the SSHRC and the
Ontario government for their financial support.

As anyone who does qualitative research knows, good quality interview data are possible only with the cooperation of the interviewees,
and we thank and acknowledge the many people who agreed to share
their expertise and insights with us, either briefly through emails and
phone surveys, or more intensively through one-on-one interviews. We
hope our book captures the main messages that they transmitted to us.

Much of the research for this book was completed with the help of
four excellent research assistants, some of whom have moved on to
academic careers and others into the "real world." Thank you to Zac
Spicer, Kari Williams, Xavier Bériault, and Jackie Demerse for their tire-
less work making phone calls, sending emails, transcribing audio files,
visiting fieldwork sites, and conducting searches for public documents.
This book could not have been completed without their help.

For Chris, much of this book was researched and written while he
was a faculty member in the Department of Political Science at Wilfrid
Laurier University. He really appreciated the fact that the department
was one of the most collegial places to work in Canada and that the university in general was very supportive of his ambitious research plans
while he was there. Thank you to his former colleagues on the fourth
floor for letting him barge into their offices to talk about his many
zany and sometimes off-the-wall ideas (thanks in particular to Loren
King and his often perplexing chalkboard expressions and equations,
Chris Anderson and his magic coffee-maker, Patti Goff, Barry Kay, Jorg
Broschek, and Sandy Irvine), the admin staff for efficiently managing
his grants, former dean of arts Michael Carroll for providing course
releases, and the university research ethics board, which always provided helpful advice and particularly quick turnarounds on applica-
tions. Thanks also to Pam Schaus, a cartographer at WLU, for designing
and putting together the maps for the book.

Jen toiled in obscurity in New York City while working in the
Urban Planning and Policy Department at Hunter College CUNY. Her
colleagues were exceptionally supportive of her unique and foreign

research. Thank you especially to Jill Simone Gross, Joe Viteritti, and Owen Gutfreund for always having their doors open and being willing to support these eclectic interests.

Many of our ideas were developed and sharpened by criticisms and feedback from a variety of academic and non-academic audiences. In particular, we thank the Departments of Political Science at the University of Guelph (where Chris was a visiting professor during the winter 2015 term) and Western University, the School of Public Administration at Dalhousie University, the academics who attended our session at the 2014 conference of the Canadian Political Science Association, and the policymakers who attended our talk in Ottawa, organized by Jodi Bruhn of Stratéjuste Consulting and John Graham of Patterson Creek Consulting. We also thank the Right Honourable Paul Martin and the three reviewers solicited by UTP, each of whom provided useful suggestions for improving our manuscript.

A special thank you to Daniel Quinlan, acquisitions editor at University of Toronto Press. Daniel is one of the best acquisitions editors in Canada and he once again proved his mettle in stickhandling another one of Alcantara's (and this time Nelles's!) manuscripts through peer review and approval with professionalism and integrity. Thanks also to the Institute of Public Administration of Canada and Patrice Dutil for including this book in their UTP book series on public management and governance and to the rest of the University of Toronto Press staff, including Wayne Herrington and our copy editor, Ian MacKenzie, all of whom helped bring this book to publication and to the wider readership of Canada.

Chris would like to thank his co-author Jen Nelles and a number of friends and mentors who helped keep him even-keeled when the project seemed to be spinning out of control: Drs Chris Cochrane (UofT), Amar Athwal (Government of Canada), Jason Roy (WLU), Graham White (his cottage), Tom Flanagan (Calgary), Rhoda Howard-Hassman (WLU), Anthony Sayers (Calgary), George Breckenridge (Shehnai Restaurant), and senior advisor of Aboriginal Initiatives at WLU, Jean Becker. Jen thanks a lot of those same people, as well as Paul Kantor (Fordham, emeritus), David Wolfe (University of Toronto), Neil Bradford (UWO), Tim Vorley (Sheffield), and Allison Bramwell (UNC), who are mentors, collaborators, and friends, and in various ways encouraged this project. She also objects to Chris's suggestion that this project was ever spinning out of control. We were obviously perfectly organized and on top of everything throughout the whole process.

Finally, none of this would have been possible without the support of our family members. Chris would like to thank his parents Eden and

Rafael Alcantara, his wife Kerry Lee Hunt, and his children Kees, Adelaide, and Anthony. A book project is an extremely time-consuming and stressful endeavour, and we thank our family members for their support, patience, and love. Jen thanks her husband Robby from the bottom of her heart and thinks that it's cute that he thought that it should be dedicated to our seven-month-old Ozzy. He's great and everything, but has been absolutely useless at proofreading and his editorial suggestions were pretty much unintelligible. So Robby, this one's for you. Thank you for making life a non-stop adventure and being the best friend anyone could ask for. Her parents Diane and Viv Nelles, and Barbara and Myron Gutmann, offered encouragement every step of the way and, most crucially, great hugs. Riker also gets a shout-out for getting me out of the house. And Geoff, Courtney, TJ, Charlie, and Nica are the best ever and have no idea how key their smiles and laughter were to fuelling the writing.

Finally, Jen would like to thank Chris – we've known each other a long time and have a partnership that has been not only productive but great fun. He managed to keep this project on track (see above) and kept the whole team moving and excited about the outcome. I have been exceptionally privileged to work with such a great friend and talented colleague.

Thanks also to Brooke Kerrigan for cover art.

Some portions of our book draw upon our previously published materials, and we thank the publishers for their permission to reuse some of those materials. These papers include Alcantara and Nelles, "Claiming the City: Cooperation and Making the Deal in Urban Comprehensive Land Claims Negotiations in Canada," *Canadian Journal of Political Science* 42, no. 3 (September 2009): 705–27; Nelles and Alcantara, "Strengthening the Ties That Bind? An Analysis of Aboriginal–Municipal Intergovernmental Agreements in Canada," *Canadian Public Administration* 54, no. 3 (2011): 315–34; and Nelles and Alcantara, "Explaining the Emergence of Indigenous–Local Intergovernmental Relations in Settler Societies: A Theoretical Framework," *Urban Affairs Review* 50, no. 5 (2014): 599–622.

A QUIET EVOLUTION

The Emergence of Indigenous–Local
Intergovernmental Partnerships in Canada

Introduction

The Indigenous–Crown relationship is a crucial component of Canada's political, legal, economic, and social identities. At the core of this relationship are the ways in which Indigenous governments and organizations interact with the governments of Canada (Abele and Prince 2003; Alcantara and Nelles 2014; Papillon 2008; Wilson 2008). This book grapples with one part of that unique and special relationship: the relationship between Indigenous and local governments. Two core questions drive this research: what kinds of cooperative partnerships exist between Indigenous and local governments and what factors explain their emergence and character?

When it comes to the Indigenous–Crown relationship, scholars, commentators, and practitioners have tended to focus on the conflicts that have occurred between Indigenous communities and the federal, provincial, and territorial governments of Canada. A plethora of academic reports, studies, and media reports, for instance, have been published on the high-profile confrontations and protests at Oka, Ipperwash, Goose Bay, Caledonia, and Gustafsen Lake, among others (Alcantara 2010; Belanger and Lackenbauer 2014; Hedican 2013; Kulchyski 2013; Morden 2013). More recently, much of the country's attention was captured for several months by the events of Idle No More, which included, among other things, a high-profile hunger strike by Chief Theresa Spence (Coulthard 2014; Kino-nda-niimi Collective 2013; Wotherspoon and Hansen 2013). Other writers have commented on and documented the disagreements and clashes in more conventional spaces, such as in the judicial and political arenas, over public policy and legal rights. The Government of Canada's efforts to address matrimonial property (Alcantara 2006; Ruru 2008) and education (Paquette and Fallon 2010) on Canadian Indian reserves, for instance, have been met with fierce criticism and opposition from some Indigenous leaders in the media and in policymaking forums. Some Indigenous groups also have a long history of suing the federal, provincial, and territorial governments of Canada for all sorts of transgressions involving their lands, economies, societies, and peoples.

From this snapshot of events and even a cursory reading of the literature (see Dickason and Newbigging 2010; Miller 2000, 2009) it would be easy to conclude that the Indigenous–Crown relationship is almost entirely adversarial and problematic. While this pessimism is certainly pervasive and somewhat justified, given Canada's history of colonialism (Abele and Prince 2003; Coulthard 2014; Irlbacher-Fox 2010; Papillon 2008), a much different story seems to be unfolding at the local level. While national and provincial media publications are filled with stories of conflict, contention, and demands, many Indigenous and local governments are quietly engaging in what seem to be highly productive and beneficial intergovernmental partnerships.

Several years ago, we published a study that analysed ninety-three publicly available intergovernmental agreements between Indigenous and local governments in British Columbia alone (Nelles and Alcantara 2011). The majority of these agreements dealt with the provision of certain municipal services (e.g., fire protection, water and sewer, and garbage removal) to Indigenous communities in exchange for some sort of yearly or fee-for-service payment. The rest of the agreements, however, were much more interesting and addressed things such as capacity building, relationship building, and even the joint management of facilities, programs, and lands. Some of the agreements also contained decolonizing language in which the local governments announced their formal recognition of Indigenous prior occupancy of the land and Aboriginal self-government.

Subsequent research has uncovered hundreds of similar documents spread across almost every province and territory in Canada, to varying degrees, illustrating that they are not restricted to British Columbia. Rather, local and Indigenous governments across jurisdictions recognize or at least assume there is value in coordinating and communicating with each other to address local and shared priorities and concerns (Walker, Moore, and Linklater 2011, 187–8). In New Brunswick, for instance, the city of Fredericton and St Mary's First Nation (which is six kilometres east of the city) have signed service agreements for the provision of water, sewer, fire, police, and other basic services rather than building new and costly infrastructure on the reserve. They have also partnered with the federal government to build a new highway through the reserve, bringing much-needed traffic and economic development to the area (Municipal–Aboriginal Adjacent Community Cooperation Project 2002, 11). In Nova Scotia, the Cape Breton Regional Municipality and Membertou First Nation have signed service agreements and have cooperated on the construction and financing of a regional road, a hospital, and commercial developments (e.g., a hotel and conference centre on Membertou-owned lands) (Federation of Canadian Municipalities 2011, 54). In Ontario, the city of Elliot Lake and Serpent River First Nation have established a Joint Relations Committee to facilitate collective dialogue and decision-making on economic issues, heritage planning, land use, land acquisition, and joint lobbying of other levels of government (Gayda 2012; Ontario Ministry of Municipal Affairs and Housing 2009). In Manitoba, the town of The Pas and the Opaskwayak Cree Nation have completed agreements on the provision of municipal services, a recycling program, a local hockey team, canine resources for the local RCMP unit, and a homelessness program (Municipal–Aboriginal Adjacent Community Cooperation Project 2002, 13). In Saskatchewan, the city of Saskatoon and the Muskeg Lake Cree Nation have not only signed service agreements, they have also established formal and informal lines of communication, such as yearly formal meetings before Christmas and frequent yet informal phone calls, letters, and emails on issues of common concern (Federation of Canadian Municipalities 2011, 96). Finally, in British Columbia, Westbank First Nation regularly appoints representatives to the Regional District of Central Okanagan's Economic Development Board. They also have signed service agreements on sewer management, economic development, transit, and animal control (Municipal–Aboriginal Adjacent Community Cooperation Project 2002, 15).

For the most part, these intergovernmental agreements and relationships have escaped the attention of academics and the media. Instead, the literature has tended to treat them as absent or tangential to the urban Aboriginal question, with some exceptions (Fraser and Viswanathan 2013; Wood 2003). Spearheaded by the authors in the highly acclaimed edited book *Urban Aboriginal Policy Making in Canadian Municipalities* (Peters 2011), much of the research on urban Aboriginals has tended to focus on the role and place of these urban Aboriginal individuals and groups and on the interface of Aboriginal organizations, broad social forces, and federal, provincial, and municipal governments in producing urban Aboriginal public policy. They focus on these issues because urban Aboriginal populations have grown substantially over the decades, not only as the result of migration, but also increasing numbers of individuals identifying themselves as Aboriginal in Canadian censuses. Scholars also focus on these issues because, although urban Aboriginals are highly diverse, at the aggregate they tend to lag significantly on a variety of socio-economic indicators (ibid.).

A variety of factors have generated this situation, one of particular relevance to this book being the absence of jurisdictional leadership from senior levels of government, which stems from their lack of knowledge or interest in Indigenous–local dynamics in Canada. A number of authors see this factor as a crucial impediment to effective public policy on urban Aboriginal problems. As Peters (2011, 24) and Andersen and Strachan (2011, 128) note, the lack of a senior-level coordinating government has led to a "patch-work of short-term, overlapping, and inefficient urban Aboriginal programs and policies" in Canada. The solution, for them, lies in federal and provincial governments clarifying their responsibilities in a comprehensive manner so that they can take coordinated action at the municipal level. Abele and Graham (2011, 34), for instance, argue, "While all levels of government are important, no other level of government has the financial resources and the reach of the federal government." In a different paper, Abele et al. (2011, 115) echo these sentiments: "The importance of the federal role is evident in all four cases … [And] changing provincial preoccupations are very important to the circumstances of Aboriginal people living in Ontario's cities."

Others have made similar arguments in their analysis of urban Aboriginal public policy in Canada (Murray 2011). In New Brunswick for instance, the federal and provincial governments have been very active in defining the relationship between municipal and Aboriginal governments. Murray (56–7) describes how senior levels of governments encouraged four types of urban-reserve relationships over the years since 1867: (1) proximity, (2) segregation, (3) eradication, and (4) trans-spatial regime in which "cities and reserves are constitutionally and economically interdependent." According to Murray (73),

A trans-spatial model of the urban–reserve relationship was brought into visibility as the federal government began praising "urban reserves" [e.g., "a reserve within or adjacent to an urban centre"] as "quiet success stories" … In New Brunswick, this model did not hinge on reserves and cities being adjacent to or geographically overlapping each other, as is the case in dominant understandings of "urban reserves." Rather, the new spatial regime was defined by interlocking constitutional and economic relationships between city and reserve. In this trans-spatial model, urban space emanated from and in conjunction with reserves. Aboriginal peoples would be in and of city and reserve. Crucially, the future of cities was deemed to hinge on an inherent Aboriginal identity tied to the reserve system. Over the latter years of the twentieth and into the twenty-first century, St Mary's reserve saw pronounced effects of this new trans-spatial discursive regime ... St Mary's band government entered into resource agreements with municipal, provincial, and federal authorities in areas such as commercial fishing ..., wood harvesting ..., land purchases ..., and taxation ... The band developed a new shopping mall and office centre that drew non-Aboriginal peoples to the reserve, a complete reversal of the nineteenth-century patterns of exchange whereby the Wolastoqiyik crossed the river to sell their goods and wares.

Senior levels of government, in the opinion of some scholars, are crucial mechanisms for facilitating more fruitful relationships between Aboriginal and municipal communities (Fraser and Viswanathan 2013; Murray 2011).

Provincial and municipal governments are also important because they can help address local concerns and fears about the duty to consult, a legal obligation that the Crown has to fulfil anytime it wishes to intrude on Aboriginal rights and title. According to Fraser and Viswanathan (2013, 3), "Municipalities do not owe a legal duty to consult First Nations since they are 'creatures of the Province.' Our research found that some municipalities clearly agreed with these sentiments, with some officials mentioning that they felt that this duty did not exist for their governments. Yet in reality, municipalities 'do hold statutory obligations since the Crown can delegate its procedural duties to third parties (as noted in the law and interpreted for the most part to be municipalities).'" In their research on the Red Hill Valley Parkway Project in Hamilton, Fraser and Viswanathan found that the municipal government had a legal duty to consult when it tried to facilitate the construction of a highway through the traditional territories of two Aboriginal communities in southern Ontario. When the city recognized this duty, negotiations proceeded more smoothly and efficiently. According to one of their interviewees, "I've always found that when municipalities understood this [duty to consult], they were quite anxious to become partners and neighbours to that type of progress" (11).

Although federal, provincial, and municipal involvement and interest are important, so too is the involvement of Indigenous actors in producing cooperation. Evelyn Peters (2011, 20–1), for instance, argues that the proportion of a city's population that is Aboriginal affects whether Aboriginal issues will receive attention from municipal governments (see also Abele and Graham 1989). On a related note, Frances Abele and her co-authors found that "generating positive municipal responses to Aboriginal issues" was largely the result of "strong, pro-active Aboriginal organizations, which took responsibility for educating politicians and bureaucrats about urban Aboriginal issues and appropriate responses to them" (Peters 2011, 24). In other words, Indigenous agency matters for spurring municipal governments to attend to Aboriginal issues and to act on them, not only in terms of internal politics, but also in terms of external relations with neighbouring communities. As we will show later in our book, some forms of Aboriginal agency are also important for producing Indigenous–local intergovernmental cooperation, but in different ways.

While governments and organizations remain crucial to the ways in which Aboriginal and municipal communities interact across and within borders, individual citizens and their perceptions of each other are also important for influencing the nature of intergovernmental relationships. Patricia Wood's (2003) analysis of the negative relationship between the city of Calgary and the Tsuu T'ina First Nation, for instance, centres on the lack of what we call community capital. Community capital, as we describe in chapter 2, refers to the presence of a shared civic identity between Indigenous and municipal communities, which has a powerful effect on the willingness of Indigenous and municipal governments to seek cooperation. Wood finds that the lack of community capital and the presence of hostility and ignorance were powerful impediments to the construction of a new road through the reserve that would better connect the southwestern parts of the city to the downtown core. According to Wood (465), "Some of the more vocal opponents of Tsuu T'ina control of the road revert to degrading stereotypes and dismissals of Natives' efforts (in general) to attain justice. The lack of respect for and recognition of the Tsuu T'ina prevents the achievement of a deal on the road. In this way, Calgarians, probably without a lot of awareness of it, reproduce a fundamental technology of colonialism: the employment of negative discourse about Natives in order to justify the dispossession of land." Later in the article, she notes, "Residents of Calgary are largely oblivious to the existence of the neighbouring Tsuu T'ina Nation, and see few connections between the fates of the communities. Many are unaware of the city's ongoing neocolonial practices, or the challenge that living beside a sprawling metropolis presents to the Tsuu T'ina. Even at City Hall, awareness of the reserve is 'ad hoc,' whereby the mayor, aldermen and bureaucrats express interest in meeting with the Tsuu T'ina usually when there is something they want" (467). This lack of a shared civic identity makes cooperation less likely between Indigenous and municipal politicians and civil servants.[1]

Despite this relatively limited attention to the topic in the literature, there seems to be a strong interest in these agreements and relationships among stakeholders and policymakers. At the 2013 "State of the Federation" conference in Kingston, Ontario, then deputy minister of Aboriginal Affairs and Northern Development Canada, Michael Wernick, spoke at length about the need for more research on Indigenous–local intergovernmental relationships. Not only were these relationships emerging rapidly across Canada, he remarked, so too was demand for knowledge of how to construct and maintain them. He believed that these partnerships could be an important tool for greatly improving not only the lives of Indigenous and non-Indigenous communities at the local level, but for also improving the broader relationship as well. Given the recent victory of Justin Trudeau and his Liberal Party of Canada at the federal level in October 2015, Indigenous–local intergovernmental relationships may become even more important as the new government puts into practice its stated intention to prioritize a nation-to-nation relationship with Indigenous communities in Canada.

Other governmental and societal actors have also demonstrated a strong interest in this topic. As we originally described it (Nelles and Alcantara 2014, 599–601), a number of federal and provincial government departments, as well as several municipal and Indigenous

---

1 Wood's paper was written in 2003. In October 2013, the Tsuu T'ina Nation and the government of Alberta signed a $275 million deal that would allow for the construction of the road in the southwestern part of the city. Although we did not study this particular partnership, it is notable that the deal was negotiated between the Tsuu T'ina Nation and the provincial government, and not with the city of Calgary.

umbrella organizations, have produced technical reports and hosted networking conferences aimed at helping local and Indigenous governments initiate and sustain cooperative intergovernmental partnerships with each other. These actors recognize that as urban regions expand their development, and as Indigenous communities increase their land base and jurisdiction through land purchases and self-government and land claims agreements, they are more likely to explore partnerships with each other and with greater frequency (Abele and Prince 2002; Alcantara and Nelles 2009; Government of British Columbia 2006; Greater Vancouver Regional District 2005). According to a Government of Ontario policy document, "Strong municipal–Aboriginal relations can assist in meeting a range of objectives, including identifying areas of mutual interest and developing joint initiatives, meeting regulatory requirements for community development, partnering on service delivery and resource management" (Ontario Ministry of Municipal Affairs and Housing 2009, 2). Similarly, other organizations such as the Union of British Columbia Municipalities agree that coordination, and the lack thereof, can have a powerful effect on neighbouring Indigenous and local communities: "Successful land use coordination can create or support joint economic development opportunities and more livable communities overall. On the other hand, lack of land use coordination can be a major source of tension and spur conflicts between neighboring communities, leading to servicing problems and to the need for dispute avoidance and resolution mechanisms. Conflicts can arise over broad community objectives or specific cross-border land use impacts such as those involving noise, smell, light (or lack thereof), increased traffic, ground water pollution, and others" (Union of British Columbia Municipalities 2000, 3).

Some Indigenous and local officials interviewed for this book told us a similar story of how intergovernmental cooperation cannot only be beneficial, but is also sometimes necessary for their communities. The potential benefits of partnership include improving programs and services (e.g., by maximizing cost-effectiveness and service efficiency); addressing complex problems that require coordination and the pooling of financial resources and human expertise; and building better relationships between adjacent communities that, as the result of growth and development, are becoming closer neighbours.

Some academics agree (Abele and Prince 2002; Walker 2008). Coates and Morrison (2009), for instance, believe that the success of Aboriginal self-government is contingent upon Indigenous communities establishing "effective and harmonious relations with local, regional, provincial/territorial, and national governments … Where there have been tensions, for example between the Kamloops Indian Band and the city government in the 1980s, progress on economic and community development came to a halt. Where levels of co-operation are high, Kamloops again providing a good example, as do Westbank, the Squamish Nation, Saskatoon, and many northern communities, major changes and advances have been possible" (118). Ryan Walker (2008) and Yale Belanger (Belanger and Walker 2009) believe that fixing the municipal–Aboriginal interface by adopting internal mechanisms of co-production and external mechanisms of cooperation with neighbouring communities is crucial to improving the socio-economic status of all municipal residents, including urban Aboriginals, in Canada.

In short, there is a lot of interest in these partnerships, because policymakers believe that Indigenous–local intergovernmental agreements may have the potential to address a variety of problems and issues facing these communities. These partnerships are also important because their growing presence may indicate the emergence of a new, underappreciated, yet optimistic trend in the ever-present and evolving relationship between Indigenous and settler communities in Canada. Yet not all communities have forged intergovernmental relationships with each other, nor are all intergovernmental relationships across Canada completely alike. Instead, our research shows that there is significant variation across communities in the nature and intensity of their intergovernmental relationships. In some cases, local and Indigenous governments have forged deep and lasting partnerships, while in other cases, the relationships are fundamentally business-oriented transactions involving municipal service provision to Indigenous communities.

In this book, our goals are to provide both a macro and micro snapshot of the intergovernmental partnerships that exist between Indigenous and local governments in Canada. To do so, we explore two main questions: (1) What types of agreements and relationships exist between Indigenous and local governments in Canada? (2) What factors explain the emergence and character of these intergovernmental agreements and relationships?

To answer these questions, we analyse the contents of all existing intergovernmental agreements that were publicly available or that we collected ourselves when our research assistants contacted every municipality and selected Indigenous communities in every province and territory in Canada. We also present and assess four case studies, each of which illustrates a particular type of intergovernmental partnership based on the degree of institutional entanglement (intensity) and frequency of inter-community interactions (engagement). Drawing on a deductively developed framework for explaining Indigenous–local collective action in settler societies (Alcantara and Nelles 2009; Nelles and Alcantara 2014), we argue that a number of factors were important for producing different kinds of cooperation in Yukon Territory, Ontario, and Quebec. More specifically, we begin our case study research by constructing a menu of factors that could influence each group's capacity and willingness to cooperate. These factors include institutions, resources, external interventions, history and polarizing events, imperative, and community capital (ibid.). From this menu of influences, we found through our empirical research that the characteristics of partnerships were a product of a unique constellation of factors, some more influential than others. Our book ends with some thoughts about how policymakers and interested parties might use these findings to initiate and perhaps sustain intergovernmental partnerships between local and Indigenous governments in Canada.

The empirical basis of the book draws partially on a data set of intergovernmental agreements gathered by a team of research assistants. Our research team contacted every municipality in Canada, first by email and then by phone, to find and record all formal and informal agreements between local and Indigenous governments. When necessary, follow-up emails and phone calls were sent and made to particular Indigenous governments when a municipal official thought that an agreement existed but was not sure. Similarly, for the case study chapters, our research assistants conducted the initial fieldwork, visiting four communities and speaking with Indigenous, local, and territorial politicians and civil servants in one territory and two provinces. In Ontario, the research team visited Sault Ste Marie, Batchewana First Nation, and Garden River First Nation. In Yukon Territory, they visited the Village of Teslin and the Teslin Tlingit Council, and the Village of Haines Junction and the Champagne and Aishihik First Nations. In Quebec the team interviewed principals in the Les Basques Regional Municipality and Malécite de Viger First Nation. As per our ethics approval, all of the interviewees were initially and automatically granted anonymity. Some chose to be identified, and their interviews are formally referenced in the book. All of the interviews, including follow-up discussions, were recorded digitally and then transcribed and analysed by the primary researchers (the authors of this book). Some interviewees requested to see our notes, transcriptions, and/or any direct quotes used in the manuscript, and these were shared and modified as necessary. Thirty officials were interviewed for this study.

Our book's objectives are both ambitious and circumspect. We seek to fill a scholarly lacuna that is also of interest to policymakers by providing a survey of existing agreements across Canada, by constructing a typology of Indigenous–local intergovernmental relationships, and by presenting a theoretically and empirically informed set of factors that seem to produce different types of Indigenous–local partnerships. However, we do not aim to provide an explicitly and fully developed normative assessment and analysis of these relationships. Rather than arguing that more-intensive and engaged relationships are better than less-intensive and engaged ones, our aim is to simply construct these categories and provide some explanations for why they exist. For some communities, perhaps a generally cooperative yet distant relationship works better and is preferable to trying to forcibly create an intense and engaged one; indeed, just because there are synergies in one area does not mean that the governments should be partners in everything. In short, we are not, in this book, trying to provide a roadmap for producing the deepest relationships possible. Instead, we explore the circumstances under which collaboration has developed and demonstrate that it can be a valuable policy option in all of its forms. We also illuminate the factors that can contribute to blocking progress on shared interests and highlighting avenues to making connections that make sense for the communities involved.

This book focuses deliberately on the conditions that enabled cooperation to develop and explores the outcomes of that cooperation only insofar as it concerns the structures and responsibilities of deepening partnerships. While in the case studies we do elaborate on the attitudes and outlooks of community leaders and members about the progress and future of their partnerships, we do not delve into their opinions of whether partnership results have been "good" or "bad." Outcomes are ultimately an important dimension to grapple with – if partnerships of this nature systematically lead to one party feeling exploited at the hands of the other, this has important implications for the study of the Indigenous–local government relationship – however, to comment on these in a robust fashion is beyond the scope of this project and detracts from our main objectives, which are to catalogue and describe the conditions of partnership formation between Indigenous governments and local authorities in Canada.[2]

In short, this book does not provide a comprehensive description and analysis of all aspects of the Indigenous–local intergovernmental relationship in Canada. When we first started this project, we had hoped to conduct normative and empirical analyses of these relationships and their outcomes, respectively, but during the course of our research we realized that these tasks were beyond the scope of our abilities. We hope that others will read this book and fill those gaps. In the meantime, we think our book provides an important contribution to a topic that clearly needs more systematic and theoretically and empirically informed research for making sense of and explaining the intergovernmental relationships that have emerged between Indigenous and local governments in Canada.

The roadmap of our book is as follows. Chapter 1 provides a macroperspective on the Indigenous–local intergovernmental relationship in Canada. It does so by analysing and surveying the many intergovernmental agreements that our research team has gathered over the last four years. Chapter 2 sketches the theoretical framework that we developed to explain the emergence of cooperation in the case study communities. Chapters 3–6 are our empirical chapters in which we present four case studies. These case studies illustrate intergovernmental relations that have low levels of intensity and engagement (e.g., chapter 3), high levels of intensity and engagement (chapter 4), and mixed levels (chapters 5 and 6). We end the book with a discussion of what our findings mean and how they might guide future researchers and practitioners interested in studying this topic further or in fostering deeper relationships between Indigenous and local governments in Canada and other settler societies.

---

2 Some readers might be dissatisfied with our explanation, so we provide additional justification for our decision here. There are two main reasons why we avoided analysing outcomes. First, to explore the degree to which agreements have been "successful" or not, or have been well received by community members for each of our 332 agreements would be a Herculean undertaking and fraught with methodological issues of bias. Secondly, outcomes do not contribute to our understanding of how partnerships emerged, the core mission of this manuscript. We hope that future research will explore whether there is a link between partnership types and outcomes, to determine if some paths to collective action create more successful outcomes than others.

Chapter One

Indigenous–Local Agreements in Canada: An Analysis of Regional and Historical Trends

While cooperative relationships between Indigenous and local authorities in Canada have garnered recent attention, the practice of establishing formally codified relationships is certainly not new. Our research has uncovered agreements dating as far back as 1928. This section explores the patterns and history of formal agreements between Indigenous and municipal authorities in nine provinces and two territories.[3] Our analysis reveals some interesting trends and differences over time and between provinces and territories. First, three provinces – British Columbia, Saskatchewan, and Ontario – are very active relative to the others surveyed. These three provinces account for over 70 per cent of all formal agreements we were able to retrieve during our research (35 per cent, 14 per cent, and 24 per cent, respectively). Second, the balance of different types of agreements negotiated varies by province. Agreements that commit the signatories to dialogue and engage in the joint governance of regional affairs, such as joint management, relationship building, and decolonization types (as opposed to municipal service delivery), have become more frequent in almost all provinces and territories. Finally, there appears to have been an acceleration of formal agreements through the 2000s, with over four times more formal agreements concluded between 2000 and 2013 than in the previous three decades, indicative of the rapid evolution of Indigenous–local relationships.

---

3 Nunavut was excluded because there are no local-level Indigenous governments in the territory. Newfoundland was included in the study, but we did not find any agreements.

This section highlights and explores these accelerating trends in Indigenous–local relationships. Following a discussion of our data collection methods we outline a typology of agreements that captures the variation in types of formal relationships that have been established between local authorities and Indigenous governments. These classifications permit us to conduct a historical and comparative analysis of evolving trends in these geographically based relationships and to highlight interprovincial differences. The ensuing analysis sets the scene for the case studies that comprise the rest of this book.

The Agreements Database: Definitions and Methodology

In order to get a sense of the landscape of cooperative agreements across Canada we built a database of the contact information for all municipalities in each province and territory. For the purpose of this study any "incorporate place" with its own government structure was considered a local government. Local officials were then contacted and asked if they had any current or former agreements with Indigenous governments. Where the municipality answered affirmatively we attempted to obtain copies of the original documents. Surrounding Indigenous authorities were also contacted to confirm the existence of agreements, or to obtain agreements (if any) in cases where local officials did not respond to our requests or declined to share their documents. Initial contact and follow-up occurred over a period of four years between 2010 and 2014.

During this period we contacted 2,262 municipalities and achieved a response rate of 80 per cent. We collected a total of 332 formal agreements. Despite the relatively large number of documents that we were able to retrieve for our database, we cannot claim to have a complete or exhaustive record of agreements to date in Canada. Some communities indicated that they had agreements but refused to share the documents with us, or did not respond to our follow-up requests. Other communities indicated that they had agreements, either current or in the past, but were unable to locate the documents themselves. Quite likely some of the communities that did not respond to any of our contact attempts also have agreements that we were unable to collect.

While we recorded the existence of all agreements (formal and informal) mentioned by local officials, only the formal agreements for which we received copies of the original text were entered into the final database for analysis. From this master list of agreements we eliminated all

Table 1.1. Totals of Agreements by Province

Province	# of agreements
Alberta	7
British Columbia	118
Manitoba	8
New Brunswick	7
Nova Scotia	14
Northwest Territories	3
Ontario	81
Prince Edward Island	1
Quebec	28
Saskatchewan	47
Yukon	18
TOTAL	332

agreements that could not be classified as cooperative agreements or that were not direct agreements between local authorities and Indigenous governments (e.g., agreements between municipal entities and the Crown to compensate for services provided to First Nations territories were excluded on these grounds). We classified any agreement that committed the signatory authorities to an ongoing and negotiated relationship as a cooperative agreement for the purposes of this analysis. Therefore, straightforward sales of land or agreements governing the collection of tax arrears were also excluded from the final database.[4]

The final database contained 332 formal agreements (see table 1.1). Finally, the full text of each agreement was reviewed by two research assistants and one of the authors and then classified according to the typology outlined below.

---

4 The land transfer agreements that we collected were typically straightforward real estate deals transferring control over land to the other party in perpetuity in exchange for a fee. These were deemed more transactional than cooperative, as the relationship between communities on the issue tended to terminate at the point of sale. Contracts governing the payment of tax arrears were also excluded, on the basis that they were usually concluded between Indigenous communities and the provincial government and similarly did not provide for cooperation or engagement beyond the point of issue resolution.

A relatively small number of communities within each province/ territory accounted for the bulk of the agreements because they had produced multiple agreements; some communities, for instance, had several agreements with the same Indigenous authorities, treating different issues, while some adopted a more comprehensive approach and negotiated multi-issue agreements. Similarly, communities surrounded by numerous Indigenous authorities often had separate agreements treating identical issues (e.g., water service) with each partner. Some communities had several agreements renegotiated periodically. Iterative agreements were counted individually. Previous research hypothesized that communities with long histories of formal agreements would progress from basic service agreements to more intensive collaborative governance arrangements over time (Nelles and Alcantara 2011). However, this hypothesis was not strongly supported by empirical evidence. It is beyond the scope of this project to rigorously trace the trajectory of every community with multiple agreements. However, our research indicates that the history of previous agreements is only one of several factors that can affect the likelihood of the emergence of collaborative governance. These factors are elaborated in the following chapter. For now, we confine the analysis in this section to the investigation of broader patterns of Indigenous–local relationships as can be discerned from the agreements database based on an analysis of the types of agreements concluded and their distribution across geographies and time.

Agreement Typology

Previous research on Indigenous–local agreements in British Columbia revealed an interesting spectrum of agreement types (Nelles and Alcantara 2011). Creating a typology of different agreements can be useful to discover and analyse patterns of relationships within and between provincial/territorial jurisdictions. Typologies can also be useful for tracking patterns of relationships over time.

Our typology is based on Nelles and Alcantara's (2011) classification of agreements into four categories: jurisdictional negotiation, relationship building, decolonization, and capacity building. We adapt this classification with the addition of two subtypes to the jurisdictional negotiation type. The six different agreement types are as follows:

Jurisdictional Negotiations

Jurisdictional negotiation agreements are the most specific of the four types. This type encompasses all agreements that involve the *transfer* of responsibilities for service, infrastructure, resources, and/or territory that lie within the jurisdiction of one party to the other and any agreements that result in *shared jurisdiction* in those areas. At their simplest, these agreements can take the form of a contract to buy services (such as snow removal or trash collection) from a municipality. More complex are those that transfer responsibility for the administration of natural resources, such as negotiations for access and water rights located in one party's jurisdiction. These agreements can take the form of legal contracts, treaties, or legislation and typically enumerate precisely the rights and obligations of each party, address issues of compensation, and outline limits and exceptions. One aim of jurisdictional negotiation agreements is to act as a reference document to govern the relationship of Indigenous and municipal/regional governments (and other levels of governments or actors, such as utilities, where relevant) as the end product of negotiations in which all the details of these relationships have been formally deliberated. Because this type of agreement represents the bulk of agreements collected from around the country, we have subdivided this category to distinguish between two types: service agreements and joint management.

Service agreements encompass the simpler form of jurisdictional negotiation and involve one party, usually the municipality, agreeing to provide a service in exchange for a fee and certain other considerations (e.g., access and autonomy of action on specific parts of the Indigenous community's territory). An example of a fairly basic service type of agreement is the fire protection agreement signed by the City of Kamloops and the Kamloops Indian Band in British Columbia on 1 April 2008. This three-year renewable agreement committed the Kamloops Indian Band to pay the City of Kamloops an annual fee (2008 fee was $436,654.42) and any overtime/enforcement costs in exchange for fire protection services, equivalent to those offered in the city, for 1,410 properties on the reserve. The agreement also committed the Kamloops Indian Band to pass a Fire Prevention By-law that "substantially incorporates the provisions of the City Fire Prevention By-Law" and applicable sections from relevant provincial legislation (City of Kamloops and Kamloops Indian Band 2008, 3–5).

Joint-management agreements are a slight variation on this formula. In these agreements the parties partner to either jointly manage the delivery of a service or administration of a resource or to jointly share the costs and/or revenues from a collaborative initiative. The main point of contrast between the subtypes is that the service-agreement type involves the full-scale delegation of responsibility for a service or project from one party to the other, whereas the joint-management variant involves some sort of shared responsibility. Both differ from the relationship-building type in their narrow focus on service delivery or the technicalities of the resource/project management rather than the establishment of a longer-term and more general partnership with respect to collective governance.

The 2011 agreement establishing the Upper Ottawa Valley Medical Recruitment Committee is an example of the joint-management subtype. This agreement committed the communities of Pembroke, Petawawa, Laurentian Valley, Bonnechere Valley, North Algona Wilberforce, the Whitewater Region, and the First Nations Algonquin of Pikwakanagan to contribute volunteers and some funding to recruit medical professionals to the region. The Upper Ottawa Valley Medical Recruitment Committee employs a physician recruiter and has put together an information portal to help mitigate the shortage of medical services in the region ("By-law to Authorize ..." 2011). Because the Indigenous partner is an equal participant in funding and management of the committee, it shares the risks and rewards of the partnership, and this narrowly focused service-provision initiative is considered an instance of joint management.

Relationship Building

Relationship-building agreements are the second most common type found within this study largely as a result of their flexibility. As the name suggests, this type of agreement is intended to be a precursor to, or a vehicle for, deepening ties between communities and their governance. These agreements are typically structured to announce the intention of Indigenous and local authorities to engage in a more sustained intergovernmental dialogue or more formal relationships in the future and outline the process by which these partnerships will be established. Occasionally these agreements structure the formal partnership and will often reference the importance of mutual recognition and respect as a basis for the partnership and contain commitments to transparency and communication.

These agreements are very common because they can run the gamut from quite vague to quite specific in outlining the processes of partnership building and the collaborative policy areas. While almost all relationship agreements announce the intention of the parties to cooperate, some of these agreements can be relatively vague on the details of how long-term intergovernmental partnerships will be created or sustained. Alternatively, they can also be quite specific on areas of mutual concern and partnership creation. As a result, this form of agreement works in a wide variety of contexts where Indigenous and municipal/regional actors want to establish cooperative working relationships or secure more formalized cooperation. In contrast to the jurisdictional negotiations type, these agreements are typically not legally binding on the signatories.

An example of this type of agreement is the memorandum of understanding (MOU) signed by the five governments of the Ktunaxa Nation[5] and eleven neighbouring local governments.[6] The MOU commits the parties to "develop strong, committed and fair working relationships between their respective governments by ensuring respectful and open communication" on all issues of mutual interest. Areas of mutual interest may include, "but are not limited to, planning for services, providing economic development opportunities, land use planning and developing infrastructure." This MOU is an important development in Indigenous–local intergovernmental relations in the area because each party recognizes "that the interests of all persons living in the communities are best served by working together in a spirit of cooperation" (Ktunaxa Nation et al. 2005, 1–2).

Decolonization

Decolonization agreements are a variant of the broader relationship-building type. In addition to the goal of establishing long-term cooperative relationships between local/regional and Indigenous authorities, decolonization agreements go further by explicitly recognizing that the

---

5 Ktunaxa Nation Council, Akisq'nuk First Nation, Lower Kootenay Indian Band, St Mary's Indian Band, and Tobacco Plains Indian Band.

6 Regional District of East Kootenay, Regional District of Central Kootenay, City of Cranbrook, City of Kimberley, City of Fernie, District of Sparwood, District of Elkford, District of Invermere, Town of Creston, Village of Radium Hot Springs, and Village of Canal Flats.

Indigenous signatories historically occupied their lands, some of which are now under the administration of municipal and/or regional authorities. In an effort to restore Indigenous influence in these lands, decolonization agreements represent a commitment to build equal and respectful relationships between local/regional and Indigenous authorities. These agreements often mark a break from the colonial past by acknowledging that there has been a "resurgence in [the Indigenous community's] population and culture and a continued assertion of their lawful and inherent rights" (Westbank First Nation and Regional District of Central Okanagan 1999, 1) and that their involvement and interest in the administration of parts of their historical territory should be reasserted. As well, these agreements may outline specific areas of cooperation and coordination and/or may announce that the intention of many of these partnerships is to establish a foundation of mutual understanding for building more integrated intergovernmental relationships.

The intergovernmental agreement between the Westbank First Nation and the Regional District of Central Okanagan is a good illustration of a decolonization agreement. This agreement, signed on 19 January 1999, recognized that "the Okanagan people of Westbank have lived in the Okanagan territory since time immemorial" and that the first non-Native people came to the area "now some 150 years" ago. As well, "the descendants of the first settlers and newcomers now insist that their governments, in keeping with the judgements of the courts, deal justly, honourably and fairly with the Okanagan and other native peoples, on the basis of equality." Finally, the parties declared that they intend "to pursue a lasting relationship based upon mutual respect and honour, in respect and recognition." Although this relationship will develop over time, the parties agreed that they would begin their relationship with biannual meetings between the chief and council of Westbank First Nation and the chairperson and directors of the Regional District of Central Okanagan to discuss and act on issues of mutual concern (Westbank First Nation and Regional District of Central Okanagan 1999).

Another example is the agreement concluded between the Haudenosaunee Wildlife and Habitat Authority, representing the First Nations Haudenosaunee and the Hamilton Conservation Authority in 2011. The agreement itself commits the parties to consult with one another on the state of the wildlife population in the region and to jointly manage populations in recognition of Haudenosaunee hunting rights. The protocol agreement states, "Haudenosaunee rights to gather, harvest and use parts of the natural world are recognized by treaties and are recognized and affirmed by the Constitution of Canada. This proto-col reflects our commitment to the implementation of those rights in a way that respects conservation, protects public safety, and fosters our mutual respect, trust and friendship," and acknowledges the sen-sitivity of the relationship by stating, "Our mutual objectives in this protocol are intended to be consistent with the principles expressed in the United Nations Declaration on the Rights of Indigenous Peoples" (Haudenosaunee Wildlife and Habitat Authority and Hamilton Con-servation Authority, 2011).

While it is common for some language of mutual respect to be included in the preamble of jurisdictional negotiation-type agreements and relationship-building documents, few go beyond acknowledgment of the authority of signatory parties. Agreements that outline the basis of a partnership with reference to historical rights and values and spe-cifically attempt to situate a partnership in the context of that history are relatively rare. Still, they are significant enough to warrant a unique place within this typology.

Capacity Building

In contrast to the previous types, capacity-building agreements are rare in this sample and represent a very different type of arrangement; capacity-building agreements commit local or regional authorities to help Indig-enous governments establish and develop their governing structures or community resources. These partnerships can be connected to the goal of developing the capacity of Indigenous communities to complete and implement formal self-government and land claims agreements or may simply involve city officials helping them to improve their governing practices, policies, and structures. In contrast to the previous two types that emphasize two-way coordination and dialogue, these agreements create knowledge transfer arrangements. This is not to say that the pro-cess of capacity building will not result in a longer-term relationship between parties. Rather, these partnerships recognize that such relation-ships require a degree of autonomy for each participant. The central purpose of a capacity-building agreement is to create the capacity for autonomy in nascent Indigenous governments or to collectively bridge skills gaps identified in Indigenous communities through training and mentorship programs. As a result, the roles and responsibilities of each party are carefully specified, although most are related to administrative issues rather than areas of mutual policy concern.

It is important to note that our definition of capacity-building agreements focuses solely on formal arrangements in which municipal governments transfer their knowledge and expertise to Aboriginal governments. This definition was deliberate, because we did not find any Aboriginal-to-municipal knowledge transfer agreements. The absence of these agreements may reflect the fact that non-Aboriginal governments, academics, and businesses have long routinely imposed Western standards of knowledge and practices on Aboriginal communities (Nadasdy 2003; Alcantara 2013), so none of these groups have felt the need to acquire Indigenous knowledge in any systematic, comprehensive, or formal way. As such, the phrase "lack of capacity" has become almost synonymous with the idea of Aboriginal communities lacking the resources and competencies that Western entities enjoy. Yet, as Howitt et al. (2013, 313) note, non-Aboriginal actors themselves suffer a capacity problem of their own: "It is widely assumed that capacity is absent only from the local, Indigenous, and community components of such [intercultural] systems and institutions ... it is often capacity deficits in government agencies, commercial interests, and non-Indigenous institutions that most dramatically affect collaborative governance of intercultural environmental systems. Significant capacity deficits include lack of knowledge, understanding, skills, and competence in basic issues of social science, cultural awareness, and locally contextualized knowledge." As time passes and the value of Indigenous knowledge and governance practices increases in the eyes of government actors, it is likely we will see new capacity-building agreements emerge in which Aboriginal actors agree to transfer their Indigenous and locally based knowledge to municipal actors.[7]

A good example of a capacity-building agreement from our sample is the Ditidaht/Pacheedaht Proposed Partnership between the Ditidaht Nation and Ladysmith: Developing Capacity for Self-Government. This agreement committed the British Columbia Town of Ladysmith to help the Ditidaht First Nations to "develop their own system of government," including governance structures, policies, and procedures.

---

7 We should note that we found no evidence that Indigenous capacity, as Howitt et al. (2013) define it, mattered for producing cooperation in our case studies. Instead, it seems that the presence of community capital was more important and may in fact capture some of the effects that the presence of Indigenous capacity may have had on the ability to cooperate.

Ladysmith administration staff also agreed to help "identify their [Ditidaht Nation] human resource needs" and provide training "in the form of supervised practical experience in addition to university or college courses." Finally, municipal staff members would "spend time with Band members at Ditinaht on an ongoing basis" to enable "the Ditidaht to have an initial level of self-government in operation within three years" (Ditidaht First Nation and Town of Ladysmith 1999, 1–2).

The employer partnership agreement (2008) between the City of Prince Albert and the Saskatchewan First Nations and Metis Relations in Saskatchewan is another example of the capacity-building type of agreement, this time focusing on community development, rather than government. It acknowledges that Indigenous persons (First Nations, Metis, and Inuit) are under-represented in the regional workforce and establishes some protocols to achieve a representative workforce. This commits the parties to work together to develop employment opportunities and career development initiatives for qualified Aboriginal applicants and for Aboriginal businesses (City of Prince Albert and Saskatchewan First Nations and Metis Relations 2008).

Analysis

This agreement typology permits us to explore historical patterns and inter-provincial/territorial differences in the development of Indigenous–local relationships in Canada. A first general observation is that formal agreements have increased over time, across all categories. Figure 1.1 breaks down each agreement type by decade between 1950 and 2014. It shows a dramatic increase in formal agreements recorded, beginning in the 1980s and accelerating through the 1990s and 2000s.

Since 2000, 264 of the agreements recorded in our database were concluded – four and a half times as many as we collected for the previous five decades. This dramatic disparity may be due to the fact that pre-1990s agreements were unknown to the officials we contacted, that agreements prior to this period had typically been informal, or that knowledge of these relationships was otherwise lost to history. However, even if these explanations can account for some temporal differences, the contemporary data support the conclusion that Indigenous–local relationships are becoming more frequent phenomena. For instance, not quite halfway through the current decade we have already recorded 102 agreements, just 60 fewer than the total for the previous decade. If these trends continue, it is highly likely that the 2010–19 period will

Figure 1.1. Agreements by Year and Type, 1950–2014

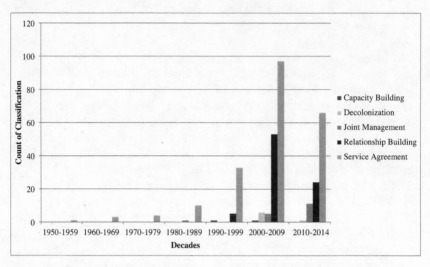

generate the most agreements of any decade to date. All of this suggests that Indigenous–local relationships, and the formal agreements that govern them, are likely to become more politically important and that we may be witnessing a significant change in attitudes and practice at this scale of political interaction.

Figure 1.1 also reveals some interesting historical patterns in the uptake of different types of agreements. Prior to the 1980s the formal agreements collected consisted exclusively of relatively straightforward service agreements. Beginning in the 1980s we begin to see joint-management types followed by an explosion of relationship building and other agreement types beginning in the 1990s. The current and previous periods have seen all types of agreements (only capacity building is so far absent from the 2010–14 sample). These patterns suggest not only that cooperative relationships are becoming more common and numerous, but that forms are also evolving. While we are careful not to attribute causality – e.g., service agreements in the past do not necessarily mean that other types of relationships between communities will necessarily evolve in the future – it seems likely that, as inter-community interactions have developed across the country, a degree of policy learning and transmission has made the conclusion of different types of agreements more likely. This is certainly so in British

Figure 1.2. Number of Agreements by Province and Agreement Type, 1950–2014

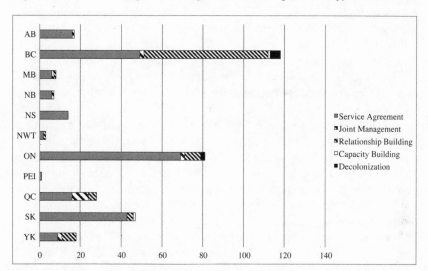

Columbia, where there have been several efforts to create a repository of agreement documents and to stimulate cooperative relationships. As well, Indigenous and non-Indigenous organizations and governments, such as the Federation of Canadian Municipalities, the Lower Mainland Treaty Advisory Board, and the Ontario government, among others, have shown a strong interest in this area, hosting a number of workshops over the years and drafting "best practices" information packets to encourage more Indigenous–local intergovernmental activity across Canada (see Nelles and Alcantara 2011, 2014).

Despite the increasing variety of agreements concluded over the past two decades, it is abundantly clear that service agreements are the most common form across all time periods and almost all geographies. Service agreements account for 67 per cent of the agreements collected in our database and exceed the next-largest category (e.g., relationship building) by a factor of almost three to one. Figure 1.2 also confirms that they are the dominant agreement type by a significant margin in every province except British Columbia.

This result is not terribly surprising: service agreements are among the most practical relationships that can bind Indigenous and local authorities and are also among the most common types of cooperative relationships between municipal governments in Canada (Spicer

2014). By virtue of their simplicity as contracts for service provision, the clear logic of economies of scale, and easily delineated obligations, such agreements are relatively easy to negotiate and tend to be politically uncontroversial.

What is less intuitive is the position of relationship building, and not the other jurisdictional negotiation variant of joint management, as the second most commonly used agreement form. While joint-management relationships commit partners to active collaboration on a specific form of service delivery or development project, the relationship-building type commits partners to work together more broadly on the joint governance of their communities. With the broader scope and frequently deeper integrative intentions of the latter form, one might expect that it would be less common. However, perhaps there are good reasons for the prevalence of relationship building versus joint management. First, relationship-building agreements are frequently vague about the specific outputs expected from the partnership. Although these partnerships commit the governments to share information or instil a duty to consult each other on issues of mutual concern, they do not always describe the structures or institutions through which these aims are to be accomplished. As a result, signing an MOU of this nature does not typically require lengthy negotiations about the division of the costs and benefits of the arrangement, nor are the resulting agreements usually legally binding. In contrast, joint-management agreements by definition require more detailed discussion of the roles, rights, and responsibilities of each participant and tend to be legally binding, if also time delimited. As these relationships often require the commitment of resources – whether financial, staffing, or time – they can be subject to more political scrutiny and public opposition. As a result, there is less risk involved in entering into a typical relationship-building agreement than a joint-management relationship. This reality is reflected in their relative frequencies.

Figure 1.2 also highlights considerable variation between provinces and territories in the use of formal agreements between Indigenous and local authorities. British Columbia stands out as the clear leader in volume of agreements concluded. Interestingly, the communities of British Columbia were not terribly early adopters of this form of inter-community diplomacy (see figure 1.3[8]). A small percentage of

---

8 Note that agreements with no date were omitted from the totals in this chart so that provincial tallies do not align perfectly with those in previous figures.

Figure 1.3. Total Agreements by Province and Year

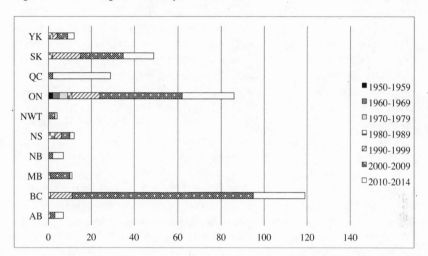

the agreements that we collected were concluded in the 1980s while the bulk of its total (90 per cent) were completed after 2000. This finding suggests that the province's current leadership on formal Indigenous–local agreements does not stem from a robust historical legacy of inter-community relations, but instead is a relatively recent development.

Ontario, by contrast, displays a much more tempered historical evolution. While 87 per cent of its agreements were concluded since the 1990s, we also collected agreements dating from every decade stretching back to the 1950s. Saskatchewan places third in the total number of agreements concluded. As with most provinces, the bulk of its agreements were also negotiated in the 1990s and onwards.

What accounts for the markedly higher rate of inter-community activity in British Columbia, Ontario, and Saskatchewan? The first and most obvious potential explanation has to do with the particularities in the geography of urban and Indigenous settlements. In all three provinces a significant number of First Nations reserves are located in relatively close proximity to local municipalities. When reserves were established, these communities may not have necessarily been as close to one another as they are today, but urban growth has, in some cases, expanded urban settlement patterns so that the boundaries of urban populations[9] have crept closer to Indigenous territory. This possibility is supported by the fact that small and mid-sized municipalities[10] of British Columbia and Ontario (and, to a lesser extent, Quebec and Saskatchewan) grew at the fastest rates in Canada between 1981 and 2011 (Statistics Canada 2011b). This urban expansion increased the importance of these places as regional centres of gravity and physically enlarged urban centres, resulting in a gradual creep towards First Nations territory; in some cases, this development impinged directly on First Nations land. These factors have increased inter-community interaction, set up circumstances where political coordination became necessary, and increased opportunities for collaborative agreements. In British Columbia a number of agreements included regional districts, a second tier of local government, among the signatories. These are depicted in the relatively larger swatches of grey in figure 1.4 and often completely encompass numerous Indigenous reserve lands. Figure 1.4 also demonstrates that the majority of agreements that we collected have been concluded between local governments and Indigenous communities that are quite close to one another. All case studies in this book explore agreements between communities that are in close proximity – that either share municipal/reserve boundaries or are within twenty kilometres of one another. In Saskatchewan a large proportion of agreements pertain to servicing and governance of urban reserves in large urban centres stemming from a similar geographical legacy. In other provinces inter-community interactions may have been tempered somewhat by a lack of opportunity.

Another potential explanation emphasizes the role of macro-legal factors, such as provincial and national legal precedents, the nature, character, and distribution of historical and modern treaties, and differences in provincial and territorial legal regimes, among others (Royal Commission on Aboriginal Peoples 1996). British Columbia, for instance, may house the highest number of Indigenous–local agreements simply because of provincial legal precedents relating to the duty to consult and the lack of historical treaties complicating local relationships. The problem with focusing on macro-legal factors, however, is that doing so does not help to explain variation in agreement and relationship

---

9 Though not necessarily their political boundaries.
10 Defined as places with population centres larger than 1,000 inhabitants. The average community size of municipalities involved in partnerships at the time of their first agreement was 39,000.

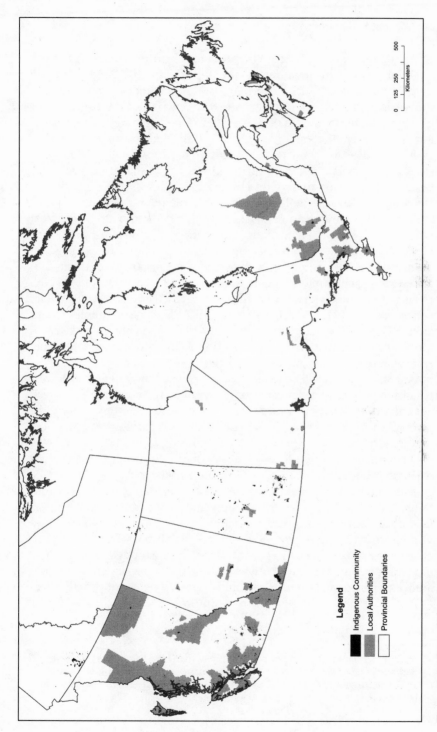

Legend

■ Indigenous Community
▨ Local Authorities
☐ Provincial Boundaries

0   125 250   500
            Kilometers

Figure 1.4. Consolidated Map

types within and across regions, provinces, and territories. Certainly we think that institutional factors are important and indeed recognize their importance by including them in our theoretical framework in the subsequent chapter, but they are only one part of the equation for generating different forms of cooperation. Given that Indigenous–local intergovernmental cooperation is almost always a localized phenomenon (because the main actors involved are local ones, rather than federal, provincial, or territorial ones), we argue that it is crucial for researchers to focus mainly on local factors, such as those relating to local capacity and the willingness of the participating actors.

Similarly, we found no evidence supporting the idea that provincial policy was crucial for generating cooperation or non-cooperation. Certainly organizations in British Columbia and the Federation of Canadian Municipalities have compiled toolkits and other resources for communities seeking to enter into cooperative partnerships with First Nations governments, but these initiatives are relatively recent (Federation of Canadian Municipalities 2011; Municipal–Aboriginal Adjacent Community Cooperation Project 2002; Tamera Services Ltd. 2002). The Ontario Ministry of Municipal Affairs and Housing has also produced documents to guide cooperation (see Ontario Ministry of Municipal Affairs and Housing 2009), but it has not consistently encouraged or facilitated the emergence of such relationships. Provincial governments overall do not appear to have been particularly engaged in encouraging this type of relationship in any jurisdiction, much less in those that are more active in partnership formation. In a handful of cases, provincial governments and/or the Crown were direct parties to agreements – typically involving the disposition of natural resources – but these were generally isolated instances.[11]

In the absence of compelling evidence to explain provincial variations in the prevalence of formal agreements we have opted instead to explore factors that led to the conclusion of agreements in a series of case studies. These help to illuminate provincial variations and to answer our primary question: what factors enable (or discourage) intergovernmental partnerships between Indigenous governments and local authorities in Canada and what can they teach us about the potential evolution of these relationships in the future?

---

11 In any case, many of these agreements were excluded from the final totals of the database because they involved federal or provincial servicing of both municipal and First Nations territories, involved land or tax transfers, or otherwise did not fit the agreement criteria specified at the beginning of the chapter.

Chapter Two

The Roots of Collective Action: A Theoretical Framework

In this chapter, we build on the literature on cooperation between local governments and regional governance (Feiock 2008; Hulst and van Montfort 2007; Nelles 2012) to develop a theoretical framework for explaining the emergence of cooperation between Indigenous and local governments in Canada. For the most part, research has focused mainly on developing a typology of agreements that have emerged in Canada (Nelles and Alcantara 2011) or on developing a framework for explaining indirect cooperation that sometimes occurs as part of other negotiation processes (Alcantara and Nelles 2009). Some have highlighted particular partnerships for their empirical or conceptual relevance to themes like the duty to consult (Fraser and Viswanathan 2013) and citizenship (Wood 2003). Others in Canada have tended to simply point out the possibility of Indigenous–local cooperation while focusing most of their attention on other Indigenous–urban dynamics (Abele and Prince 2002; Coates and Morrison 2009; Peters 2011; Walker 2008). The comparative literature on this topic is virtually non-existent, with only one published article examining the ways in which U.S. tribal and municipal officials sometimes work together to cultivate policy and political expertise to further their goals (Evans 2011). This chapter builds on this literature by identifying a range of factors that may encourage the emergence of Indigenous–local intergovernmental partnerships in Canada.

At the core of our theoretical framework is our contention that both political capacity and political willingness are important determinants of cooperation and that these are shaped by the interaction of six key factors: institutions, resources, external intervention, history and polarizing events, imperatives, and community capital.

Each of these factors may contain the seeds of cooperation or provide impediments to partnership formation, depending on the context. We expect that in any given case some factors will support collective action, while others will oppose it, and yet others may not have any effect at all. We do not expect that there will be a configuration of factors that will *always* result in cooperation or that the framework will be useful a priori to predict the outcomes of hypothetical partnerships. Rather, it is a tool for understanding and explaining how local contexts combine with these factors to produce the partnerships that they have. Of the six factors, only community capital is likely to have a consistently positive effect on the emergence of cooperation. The application of this framework to the four case studies presented in the following chapters bears this hypothesis out and has important implications for policymakers seeking to enable and encourage this type of cooperation in the future. A deeper understanding of the variable effect that each of the other six factors can have on partnership formation may also provide valuable insights into why attempts at different forms of cooperation have failed and offer keys to progress in the future.

Background Considerations: Cooperation and Comparability

This theoretical framework begins with the assumption that in any case examined, there has been an opportunity to collaborate – e.g., a problem that could have been solved by Indigenous–local collective action – and that all parties to the partnership have the *potential* to benefit from the relationship. That is, this framework is not intended to explain inaction where cooperation may benefit only one party. Rather it is formulated to explore why cooperation emerges, or does not, in areas where a *potential* mutual benefit from collective action has been *identified* and is *recognized* by all parties.[12]

A second caveat is that although we have adapted our approach mainly from the literature on local intergovernmental relationships, we want to emphasize that we recognize that Indigenous governments are

---

12 Note that this doesn't mean that there must be consensus between the cooperating parties about what the mutual benefit *is*, just that both parties perceive that mutual benefit is possible.

not the same as other Canadian local authorities, nor would we argue that they should be treated as such. However, they share a number of similarities that justify the use of the intergovernmental model with modifications sensitive to key differences. From a structural point of view, municipal and (most) Indigenous governments (e.g., band council, Indian Act communities) in Canada are similar across a number of dimensions. They are both forms of government to whom political power has been devolved in order to administer a legally bounded territory, to provide services to their constituents, and to participate in the localized implementation of policies developed at senior levels of government. Both forms of government consist of democratically elected councils and leaders and, since the 1988 amendment of the Indian Act, wield similar revenue-raising and economic development tools. Finally, while Indigenous governments are often involved in policy areas and challenges that are distinctive from non-Indigenous communities, a large proportion of the daily concerns that occupy municipal politicians are also shared by Indigenous leaders. Yet it is important to note that many Indigenous leaders reject the characterization of their governments as municipal, maintaining that Indigenous self-government and self-determination are inherent rights that they have always had and made use of long before the arrival of Europeans and that continue to exist today.

The key structural differences between the two types of government concern their decision-making structures, constitutional status, and status of relationships with other levels of government. First, while decision-making processes in municipal governments across the country are relatively consistent, there is considerable variation between bands in their internal decision-making practices. As a result, it is important to take these important differences into account when analysing political outcomes in a comparative context. Second, local and Indigenous governments in Canada fall under the constitutional purview of different levels of government: provinces are responsible for municipalities ("Constitution Act," 1867 §92.8), while the responsibility for "Indians, and Lands reserved for Indians" (§91.24) belongs to the federal government.[13] Furthermore, their roles are established by

---

13 It is important to note that while Indigenous constitutional and legal orders exist and operate within many Indigenous communities, they have yet to be recognized in any meaningful or practical way within the constitutional framework of Canada.

different sets of legislation. First Nations issues are governed largely by the Indian Act and other pieces of federal legislation, while local governments are governed by provincial municipal acts and, on occasion, specific local charters. On a practical level this means that each form of localized government – Indigenous and non – are subject to very different sets of legal frameworks and have hierarchical and historical relationships with different parts of provincial and federal bureaucracies. Finally, while the legal status of local governments in Canada has been fixed since the Baldwin Act (1849), the legal status of individual Indigenous communities varies by province, depending on their treaty and self-government status. While some Indigenous groups have concluded land claims and self-government negotiations with the Crown, there are still a significant number that are in the process of concluding, have failed to establish, or have not yet attempted to negotiate final agreements (Alcantara 2013). Treaty and self-government status can therefore be an important institutional distinction between Indigenous groups, and accord rights that are distinctive from those of local governments. Furthermore, the treaty experience is an important historical context in of itself, which may profoundly shape the propensity of Indigenous groups to trust and enter into further relationships with Canadian governments (ibid.).

Despite these important differences, it is possible and fruitful to analyse relationships between Indigenous and municipal governments using a single theoretical framework. Even analyses of inter-municipal relationships that fail to recognize differences between the partners do so at their own peril. Our aim here is to construct a framework that incorporates these main distinctions between different types of authorities, be they Indigenous or municipal. We expect that these relationships will display many of the same attributes observed in the inter-municipal governance literature: a wide variety of variables conspire to encourage or discourage partnerships, but only a few of these variables will be predictive.

The Foundations of Cooperation: Capacity and Willingness

We argue that the decision to enter into a partnership is determined by two important factors: the *capacity* of actors to enter into such an arrangement, and their *willingness* to do so. *Capacity* is defined as what partners are permitted to do by the structures that govern them as well as what they are able to do with the tools at their disposal. *Willingness*, by contrast, is the degree to which actors are disposed to invoke their capacities to act. Where actors lack the capacity to enter into partnerships, it is not surprising that they do not. However, where partners are not significantly constrained by rules or resources (among other things), the emergence of cooperation is still not assured. It is therefore important to consider the factors that affect the political will to sacrifice a degree of local autonomy,[14] however small, to collective action. We contend that in cases in which all relevant actors have sufficient capacity to enter into a partnership – recalling the assumption that all partners perceive potential benefit from such an arrangement – the emergence of the partnership depends on the political will of each actor to engage in a cooperative relationship. One could even further imagine that sufficient political will could, in fact, overcome capacity barriers to cooperation by actors lobbying to change legal restrictions or similar phenomena. Whatever the status of capacity, willingness is key. The following theoretical framework introduces six factors that can influence the capacity and willingness of actors to engage in collective action. Each factor can conceivably affect both the capacity *and* willingness of actors, but we think they can be more usefully conceived as occupying a spectrum based on their tendency to affect one to a greater degree than the other. This spectrum is illustrated in table 2.1.

The Six Elements of Cooperation

Our theoretical framework categorizes the factors that may affect the emergence of cooperation between Indigenous and municipal governments into six groups. These groups are discussed in the order in which they are arrayed on the capacity-willingness axis (table 2.1). For each empirical case study, researchers must determine the effect of each category on the development, or not, of cooperation. While quantitative research using this framework is not impossible, we have envisioned and constructed it primarily as a guide to qualitative investigations.

---

14 Some readers might argue that this statement is inherently normative in some way. Our view, however, is that cooperation inherently involves some sort of diminishment of autonomy when compared to simply engaging in the action independent of others. Cooperation, generally speaking, involves at least minimal coordination of timing and action with another actor.

Table 2.1. Capacity–Willingness Spectrum

	Factor	Definition	Example
Willingness Capacity	Institutions	The rules and norms that govern decision-making processes	Executive autonomy; council autonomy; legal status of Indigenous governments
	Resources	The means available to engage in collaboration	Financial resources, but also time, expertise, staffing, and infrastructure
	External intervention	Actions by other (senior) levels of government	Direct intervention through involvement in agreements, or indirect intervention through policy changes that affect incentives, capacity, etc.
	History and polarizing events	The history of relationship between communities or sudden events (endogenous or exogenous) that change the incentive structures of actors	Successful partnerships in the past may encourage new partnerships in the future; bad blood can sour relations; natural disasters, perceived slights, the entrance (or exit) of a key actor
	Imperative	The perception of a shared problem and the urgency of the need for a collaborative solution	The perception of shared (although not equal) benefit from cooperation
	Community capital	Shared civic identity – understanding that, despite differences, the two (or more) communities are part of a shared region; social integration	Integration across the regional workforce, diversity in the leadership of civic organizations; presence of leaders who champion the shared region

Each group of variables, and the individual variables within each group, will have a positive, negative, or no effect on cooperation. Researchers have the additional option to qualify their assessment with terms such as *strong* or *weak*, *major* or *minor* to distinguish differences in magnitude. In the case studies that follow we provide clear examples of how the framework can be applied.

In case study research there is often an explanation for success or failure that stands out immediately and that has been adopted as a consensus by popular media and opinion. One primary function of this framework is to encourage researchers to explore as many of the potential impacts on cooperation as possible in order to better understand the interaction between forces that produce certain outcomes. While it is possible that the same explanation will emerge as dominant upon deep analysis, this framework may still be useful to illuminate other minor, or even significant, contributing factors.

That said, in presenting this framework we make no claims to absolute comprehensiveness, nor do we expect that it will be applied unmodified by other researchers. As a framework it provides a conceptual approach to the question of Indigenous and local government cooperation and suggests an array of factors that our research indicates has the potential to influence this type of behaviour. In the following section we discuss each variable group and subtype in turn. We particularly note the degree to which each influences capacity and/or willingness and hypothesize the potential impact – positive or negative – on cooperation. As the following analysis will show, many factors can have positive *or* negative consequences for cooperation, depending on local contexts. It is important to stress that while we identify factors that can encourage or discourage collective action, we are careful to make no normative statements about the appropriateness of these conditions.

Institutions

Institutions are the rules and norms (Hodgson 2006; North 1990) that govern the decision-making processes of local government and Indigenous actors. Institutions typically affect the degree to which actors are able to enter into specific types of agreements. However, the impact of institutional constraints can certainly also affect their willingness to do so. Among the most important institutional factors that can affect the emergence of cooperation are executive autonomy, jurisdictional autonomy and functions, treaty status, and decision-making processes. Many of these are interrelated – e.g., executive autonomy and decision-making processes – so it is likely that the effects of those variables will track together.

The degree to which executives are empowered to make decisions on behalf of their constituents without rigorous ratification processes can liberate leaders to make commitments to partnerships. However, this autonomy can be a double-edged sword. Where leaders are committed to cooperation, executive autonomy can ease the negotiation process by reducing the number of actors who need to be involved and assuaged. Where one or more empowered executives oppose cooperation, however, they can also be exceptionally powerful in blocking progress. It is therefore difficult to predict whether a relatively autonomous executive will be an advantage or barrier to cooperation. In the Canadian context, local executives are typically quite weak and are rarely empowered to commit their bureaucracies without council approval. Weaker autonomy does not necessarily preclude cooperation but can add to the challenges of reaching a mutually beneficial agreement. The degree of executive autonomy of Indigenous governments, however, can vary significantly from case to case. Executives may be bound by consensus decisions of the council or may enjoy more political freedom (Alcantara and Whitfield 2010). For most First Nations under the Indian Act, for instance, the powers of the chiefs are constrained by the need for band council approval, and so executive autonomy is circumscribed, at least formally. Informally, however, executive autonomy varies from band to band, especially in communities where certain families dominate local band politics. In either case, there is likely to be a degree of asymmetry in executive autonomy that may prove frustrating to the party with fewer internal barriers to agreement. As discussed above, the decision-making processes within local and Indigenous governments may be quite different. Both the types of decision-making processes and the asymmetry between them can block the emergence of cooperation. Where more individuals and interests are involved in negotiations it can be more difficult to secure collective action (Olson 1965). Time is also a factor associated with this variable. Where motions to approve collective action must pass through more steps – as though subcommittees or internal reviews – the additional time required to get a deal done may try the patience of the speedier actor. Lengthy decision-making processes also pose the risk that what is approved may contain several modifications to the original agreement, which may necessitate another round of bilateral negotiations to determine if the changes are mutually acceptable (Fraser and Viswanathan 2013, 13).

The legal status of the Indigenous government relative to others in the Canadian federation can also complicate cooperation. Treaties and self-government agreements typically set out and clarify the lands, rights, and responsibilities of Indigenous governments (Abele and Prince 2003; Papillon 2008). Therefore, where treaties and self-government agreements exist, Indigenous governments operate in a uniquely settled and relatively transparent political space. Where treaties and self-government agreements are not in force, or are in the process of negotiation, there may be a measure of uncertainty about the extent and limits of Indigenous jurisdiction. This legal uncertainty can make cooperation with other governments more difficult to achieve (Abele et al. 2011, 100, 109), particularly in cases where treaties and self-government agreements are being negotiated (Alcantara 2013). From another perspective, the uncertainty generated by the negotiation process (or lack thereof) may induce Indigenous governments to seek local partners to build political capital for future negotiations or extend their political reach on issues affecting their constituents.

Resources

Indigenous and municipal authorities typically govern with relatively few resources, particularly outside of the larger cities and settlements. Where local and Indigenous authorities have discretionary funds to support joint projects, cooperation will likely be easier to establish. The availability of financial resources can be important, even when partnerships do not require significant monetary contributions. Even in the most ad hoc arrangements, the process of meeting and coordination is not without costs (e.g., travel, renting conference facilities, or providing refreshments). The ability and willingness of each party to share in those costs can be significant to the conclusion of a successful agreement (Bel and Warner 2015; Hawkins and Carr 2015; Kwon and Feiock 2010).

In addition to financial and administrative resources, time and expertise can also influence cooperation. For instance, support staff may not be reliably available to manage communication and project implementation in governments – Indigenous and municipal – with small or part-time staffs. Similarly, the time commitment required by elected officials and representatives to conclude even simple agreements can be onerous. Where legal or specialized knowledge is required, local and Indigenous officials may lack the expertise to proceed without external (and often expensive) assistance (see Alcantara 2013; Evans 2011).

Every political decision entails a set of costs. Even the preliminary discussions about the potential for partnerships are not entirely free. All actors shoulder some burdens – financial, administrative, or temporal – in the process of coming together and in maintaining the partnership. The extent to which each partner is able to spare the necessary resources can be an important factor in the emergence of collective action. The more discretionary resources each partner has, the less likely that each will cite this factor as a barrier to cooperation. However, it is also possible that where actors enjoy relatively high levels of resources the arguments about the potential benefits of collective action that accrue from, for instance, economies of scale, may hold less weight. In this example an actor may choose to bear a higher cost to deliver the service alone in exchange for the benefits of greater autonomy. Finally, even where the absolute stock of resources is relatively large, context plays an important role in shaping the willingness of an actor to pool those resources for collective action. Communities with lots of resources may also face elevated demands such that collective action ranks lower relative to other local (or more politically advantageous) issues and competing claims. As a result, the absolute stock of resources alone, while an important factor, may be a poor predictor of collective action and thus highlights the importance of mapping the broader context within which weaker and stronger forms of cooperation take place.

External Intervention

Occasionally senior levels of government become a factor in the construction of regional partnerships between municipal and Indigenous governments (Gayda 2012). Provincial or federal governments in Canada, for instance, can influence the formation of local partnerships in two ways: directly, through direct participation in the negotiation process or indirectly through policy actions that affect local decision-making. The first and more activist instance is the easiest to identify and analyse. In these cases the senior level of government either leads the formation of the partnership or is a member. This scenario is more typical in areas where local and senior level jurisdictions intersect, as is the case with environmental governance (e.g., managing watersheds; see Greitens, Strachan, and Welton 2013). Whether a leader or simply a participant in the partnership, a senior level of government can bring enticements (such as resources) to the local participants, add weight to an issue and attract the participation of local actors, or impose requirements for local participation. All of these can significantly alter the decision-making processes of local actors towards cooperation (Fraser and Viswanathan 2013, 8; Gayda 2012).

Indirect influence by senior levels of government can be more difficult to detect, but can also be significant in promoting (or discouraging) partnership formation. For instance, a provincial government may pass new legislation requiring new environmental protections for locally owned land. In order to economically satisfy this additional burden, local authorities may seek partnerships with other localities or governments. Senior levels of government can also intervene by providing resources to one or both partners to support local involvement in a given policy area (Moore, Walker, and Skelton 2011, 34). Where resources are augmented, this may increase the propensity of actors to cooperate. Similarly, resources or capacity can be withdrawn. While these more indirect influences are difficult to predict, they can provide significant and usually unintended motivation for (or barriers to) local cooperation.

History and Polarizing Events

Partnerships seldom emerge in a vacuum – they are the product of, and conditioned by, the historical context in which they were nurtured. As such, the success of previous partnerships and the historical relationship between Indigenous and local authorities can profoundly affect the willingness of partners to engage in collective action. Similarly, triggering or polarizing events can stimulate cooperation where there were none previously (or derail existing partnerships).

The success or failure of partnerships between local actors, even in unrelated policy areas, can be powerful indicators of the likely behaviour and trustworthiness of the parties involved. Where partnerships have been successful, it is more likely that local actors will be willing to engage in another. Where previous partnerships or negotiations have failed, the actors are likely to have negative memories of the experience and may be wary of another attempt.

Even where no other partnerships have been implemented or attempted, the historical relationship between local and Indigenous authorities will influence the decision-making process. A history of discriminatory policies, failure to consult Indigenous representatives on a development project, failure to pay for services on time, or an outspoken personality in either group can sour relations between local authorities and affect the perceptions of contemporary actors, even when those people, policies, or developers are long gone (Alcantara and Nelles 2009; Zeemering 2008). Rightly or wrongly, history has the potential to be a powerful barrier to cooperation (or even contemplating cooperation). While negative history is not insurmountable, the negative perceptions that it generates can be very difficult to overcome.

Polarizing events are any kind of dramatic change that shifts the calculus of any of the potential partners with regards to their capacity or (more often) willingness to engage in collective action. These can be the product of individual decisions (such as the decision to implement a specific policy) or completely unpredictable events (such as natural disasters) (Birkland 1997). A polarizing event can be a reason for a partnership to form, it can lead to the dissolution of what appeared to be successful negotiations, or it can lead to the dissolution of a partnership. As with external intervention, polarizing opportunities can be direct or indirect.

Direct polarizing events are those that are initiated by the actors involved in partnership negotiations themselves. If one partner decides to act in a way that will aggravate partners, whether it is related to the substance of the partnership or not, this can constitute a polarizing event and introduce complications into negotiations or threaten existing agreements. For instance, if an Indigenous government decided to build an attraction on its land that will compete with attractions in neighbouring municipalities, this may sour negotiations on other issues, regardless of whether or not they are related. Knowingly pursuing policies that will be unpopular with (potential) partners can, intentionally or not, destabilize relationships and can be construed as an act in bad faith (Alcantara and Nelles 2009).

Indirect polarizing events are those initiated by actors outside of the partnership, or through an act of God, that significantly changes the incentives for cooperation. For instance, cooperation motivated by a change in legislation (such as the environmental example given above) may be negated by the emergence of a not-for-profit willing to fund local compliance. This would remove the immediate need for at least one of the actors to cooperate on this issue. Similarly, a natural disaster, such as the flooding of a nearby river, could prompt Indigenous and local authorities to partner for flood management and recovery. In this case a shared threat can function as a positive polarizing event.

A significant feature of polarizing events is that their impact on partnerships can vary substantially, their influence can be either positive or negative, and they can be relatively difficult to foresee. An unpopular political decision by one of the actors may not necessarily scuttle a partnership, but it can make it more difficult. The emergence of an alternative to cooperation (such as a new source of funding) can eliminate the necessity for collective action altogether. As such, polarizing events can be exceptionally powerful in partnership formation (or barriers to partnership formation).

Imperative

In most partnerships the motivations for cooperation and the benefits that each partner receives from cooperation vary. In some cases a partnership that is merely convenient for one partner may be a necessity for the other(s). This asymmetry of "need" or imperative for cooperation is not necessarily a factor in negotiations. However, it is possible to imagine a case where one actor, or several, badly needs the cooperation of the others. When the stakes are much higher because of the costs of failure, a partner may be willing to overlook other mitigating circumstances (e.g., a history of bad blood, or the time it will take to get a deal done). While these situations are most likely relatively rare, the imperatives (i.e., the pressure to get a deal done) that local decision-makers face in approaching partnerships can be important to understanding the emergence or failure of cooperation (Belanger and Walker 2009, 132). Imperative can alternatively be referred to as the stakes involved in partnership. Where the stakes are high for one or all partners, collective action may be a more likely result, regardless of other barriers. Where imperatives are weak, partners may be less willing to come together, even where there is a potential for mutual benefit – other issues, other solutions, or plain old inaction can be more compelling than collective action in this context.

Community Capital

Community capital is a combination of attributes of an urban region, and its peripheral settlements, that form a shared civic identity. These are the factors that form a feeling that municipal and Indigenous communities are "in this together" in the minds of residents, political representatives, and groups within the region. While Indigenous and non-Indigenous communities may have separate governing structures, community capital blurs these jurisdictional boundaries to unite these groups as residents of a unique and shared – if politically fragmented – territorial space.

Community capital is unique among the variables listed here, in that its effect on the emergence of cooperation will always be positive. While government intervention and institutions, for instance, can have either positive or negative effects on cooperation, depending on the context, community capital will always have a positive (although varying in degree) influence on the emergence of partnerships. As a result, we expect that partnerships between Indigenous and municipal governments will be more likely to be proposed and successfully negotiated in the presence of a strong and shared civic identity.

This variable is also one of the most complicated to operationalize. It is difficult to measure collective identity and shared vision. In order to put some flesh on these conceptual bones we use a series of proxies that function as indicators of the depth of community capital. Principle among these is the degree of integration, number of inter-community networks, and links between regional leaders.

Social integration between Indigenous and municipal communities can be an important indicator of mutual respect and shared identities. Where there is regular interaction between communities, it is more likely that this sense of identity will emerge. Non-political inter-community networks are also an important indicator of regional integration. Where more local civic groups are actively inclusive in their catchment areas, it is more likely that a shared conception of community and vision have been established. Finally, community leaders who are active champions of inclusive civic engagement are one of the most visible dimensions of community capital. Where community leaders vocally pursue the joint interests of Indigenous and non-Indigenous communities, they are likely to be reflecting the views of others in the region and articulating a vision supported by a regional coalition, if not a regional consensus.

In the case studies we rely on the perception of the interviewees of these three dimensions to determine the degree of community capital and its effect. We rely on perceptions rather than objective measures because fundamentally, political leaders are at the core of Indigenous-local intergovernmental partnerships. Political leaders who perceive the presence of strong community capital are more likely to be open to cooperative proposals from their counterparts in neighbouring communities. It is logical to expect communities that seem to share a civic identity to be more welcoming of proposals that bring their governments together, compared to communities who lack such an identity.

It is important to note that pre-existing agreements are excluded from this variable in order to avoid the trap of tautology, where the presence

of political partnerships explains the emergence of new political partnerships. While previous formal partnerships may be significant, they
are considered as historical factors rather than evidence of community
capital. We argue that the social ties that are built between communities as a by-product of organic and ordinary interactions form the basis
of a shared identity that can lead to a greater willingness of political
actors – and their constituents – to consider formal political partnerships between Indigenous and local governments for their collective
benefit. This collective identity may, in some cases, be powerful enough
to overcome barriers imposed by the previous five factors that might be
intractable in more divided communities.

We have also deliberately chosen to use the language of "capital" to
anchor this concept. This is a nod to the conceptually related concepts
of social capital (Coleman 1988; Evers 2003; Lin 2001; Putnam 2000) and
civic capital (Henton and Melville 1997; Nelles 2012; Potapchuk and
Crocker Jr, 1999; Wagner 2004; Wolfe and Nelles 2008) that also rely
on the presence of networks, civic engagement, and trust to explain
phenomena such as collective action and innovation. While our formu-
lation certainly owes an intellectual debt to these predecessors, community capital is a unique and specialized variation on their conceptual
themes. Perhaps most importantly, the term *capital* implies a resource
that can be accrued (or lost) and used to productive purposes (or squan-
dered). Community capital will not inevitably increase over time, nor
is it immune to depreciation if community interaction wanes. As such,
it is important to judge the emergence of each partnership relative to
community capital at that point in time rather than through the lens of
the present.

These six dimensions of our theoretical framework were envisioned
to provide a better understanding of the emergence of relationships
between Indigenous and municipal governments. In the chapters that
follow we explore the influence of each of these factors on the emergence of four different types of Indigenous–local intergovernmental
partnership.

Four Types of Cooperation: A Roadmap for
Applying the Theoretical Framework

In our field research we encountered a wide variety of agreement types
and relationship configurations. For instance, while all of the communities discussed in the previous chapter have an agreement (and

sometimes multiple agreements) in place, the relationships that have evolved between Indigenous and local authorities in the course of negotiating and sustaining these agreements exhibit considerable variation. In this section we propose a framework to distinguish four main types of cooperative relationships based on variations in the frequency of inter-community engagement and the institutional intensity of existing partnerships. The case studies presented in the chapters that follow provide examples of each different type of relationship and offer an opportunity to analyse the effect of the six factors on different relationship types.

We propose that the relationships between Indigenous and municipal authorities can be differentiated along two dimensions. The first dimension is the degree of engagement between the parties. Here, the focus is on how frequently the parties communicate with one another on the topic of the agreement(s) and/or to resolve other issues of mutual concern. Communication may take the form of regular and formal face-to-face meetings, less formal but routine phone and email contact, or ad hoc meetings as issues arise. The key to this dimension is not necessarily the form of contact, but the frequency. Higher frequencies of all types of communication may indicate the institutionalization of information exchange, higher levels of mutual respect, and recognition of the interdependence between communities. They may also indicate conflict, but to the extent that communication levels are higher, this might also mean that the two parties are still talking and attempting to seek resolution. In either case, we equate higher levels of communication as a sign of deeper engagement with the other authority.

The second dimension of our classification of relationships is related to the intensity of Indigenous–local agreements. We deem partnerships to be low intensity if their formal agreements are limited to standard service-delivery agreements, and high intensity when they address issues of decolonization, set up processes for information sharing, or require joint investments or joint management of resources. Intensity here is a measure of the degree to which both parties are required to sacrifice individual autonomy for the achievement of collective goals. Service agreements, which typically bind the parties in a service provider–client relationship in which a service is provided by one in exchange for a fee from another, require relatively minimal sacrifice by either party. A commitment to mutual consultation in an issue area, however, can limit the autonomy of the parties to proceed without heeding the concerns of the other. A commitment to partner on joint management further erodes

Table 2.2. Relationship-Type Matrix

	Intensity	
Engagement	High	Low
High	Strong synergy	In the loop
Low	Agreement-centred	Business as usual

that autonomy and requires consensus building and even perhaps the pooling of resources. As such, the characteristics of the agreement negotiated, and the practices that emerge from them, can also tell us much about the commitment to partnerships and the underlying relationships between the communities. As with engagement it is possible to evaluate informal, uncodified, relationships using this framework.

These two dimensions can be arranged on a matrix resulting in four distinctive types of cooperation: cooperation characterized by (1) high intensity and frequent engagement – strong synergy; (2) high intensity and infrequent engagement – agreement-centred; (3) low intensity and high engagement – in the loop; and (4) low intensity and low engagement – business as usual. These four types are depicted in table 2.2.

Strong synergy relationships are those where agreements have resulted in a highly institutionalized partnership – such as the joint management of a resource, facility, or program or a (semi-)permanent association with shared leadership – and where intergovernmental communication within and outside of the partnership is relatively frequent. Often, highly institutionalized partnerships involve regular meetings. Depending on the frequency of those meetings, communication may be considered quite high (e.g., monthly or weekly). Where formalized meetings happen less often (e.g., annually or biannually) informal communication may still be quite frequent. As such, we explore degrees of both formal (agreement-related) and informal contact between governments to determine whether a community fits within this category.

Agreement-centred relationships are, as the name suggests, focused almost exclusively on the agreements at their core. In this variant, parties have established a relatively high-intensity partnership with few formally scheduled meetings or other interactions. While communities typically get along amiably, overall this type of relationships produces very little communication outside of what is prescribed by the partnership. Note that "little communication" does not imply that no other interaction takes place, rather that there are no regular informal exchanges outside of what is courteous. This lower level of engagement may stem from the perception by all parties that intergovernmental interaction within the confines of the partnership is sufficient to individual community needs. Actors may occasionally recognize opportunities for further collaboration but may, or may not, seek to deepen contacts to execute on that vision.

Communities with lower-intensity partnerships – such as service agreements – may still have relatively high levels of intergovernmental interaction. In these in-the-loop relationships the agreements are important connections between the communities but are not the only venues for interaction. In these relationships officials informally keep each other "in the loop" and informed of policies and occurrences that might have a bearing on the other government's business. While some communities have opted to formalize this kind of information exchange with formal MOUs, others see no need for such arrangements when informal communication serves them adequately. As a result, we do not expect that this particular type of relationship will necessarily lead to more intense cooperation, although that is certainly a possibility.

Finally, communities involved in business-as-usual partnerships tend to treat intergovernmental relationships as business transactions and do not engage with one another beyond the relatively minimal requirements of the partnership or what is neighbourly. The agreements are usually limited to the provision of services by one party to another and do not require much communication other than periodic renegotiations and cash transfers. In this type of partnership the business of each community is regarded as separate, and very little (even informal) attention is paid to the interests or concerns of the other outside the boundaries of the agreement.

While in each case study we are interested in what led to the specific agreements negotiated, we also explore how each factor has shaped, and continues to shape, general relationships between the communities as described by this typology. One advantage of this framework is that it allows us to go beyond the agreements themselves to explore the degree to which communities actually interact in support (or in contravention) of their partnership.

The approach also allows for the possibility that local and Indigenous authorities have developed institutionalized relationships *in parallel with or in lieu of* formal agreements and that formal agreements have emerged from these less visible relationships.

Applying the Framework

In what follows we detail four case studies that stood out from the agreements studied in the previous chapter. Each case represents a specific variant of cooperation – one for each cell of the matrix. In each case we assess the impact of the six factors of our theoretical framework on the resulting partnership(s). The concluding chapter discusses findings from a comparative analysis of these cases.

The four case studies highlighted in the following chapters are (1) the City of Sault Ste Marie and its relationship with Batchewana First Nation and Garden River First Nation in northern Ontario; (2) the Village of Teslin and the Teslin Tlingit Council in Yukon Territory; (3) the Village of Haines Junction and Champagne and Aishihik First Nations in Yukon Territory; and (4) the Regional Municipality of Les Basques and Malécite de Viger First Nation in Quebec.

We chose these cases for a number of reasons and by sifting through the collected agreements to identify potential Indigenous–local partnerships to fill the four boxes of our matrix. Our main case selection criterion was that there had to be at least one completed agreement between the Indigenous government and the local authority. Recall that a primary goal of this book is to describe and analyse existing Indigenous–local intergovernmental relationships in Canada, so we do not examine cases in which cooperation was completely absent. We also chose cases that varied according to location (e.g., two provinces and one territory) to capture potential jurisdictional effects and cases that contained variation in governance structures; two of the Indigenous communities have signed comprehensive land claims and self-government agreements, and three of the communities operate under an Indian Act band council structure. There was also considerable variation on the local side, with two cases involving village governments, one with a regional-tier government, and one municipality. In some ways, therefore, our case selection reflects a *most-different systems* logic (Przeworski and Teune 1970), with the common element among the cases being the presence of some sort of intergovernmental agreement. Our hope is to use the differences inherent in these cases to help identify the factors that seem to encourage Indigenous–local intergovernmental cooperation across a variety of institutional and geographical contexts in Canada.

Some might argue that our choice of case studies is problematic because the communities are unique and not representative of the majority of Indigenous–municipal communities in Canada. We agree to some extent with these criticisms, but we also note that it is next to impossible to choose any set of cases that are nationally representative, given the unique nature of Indigenous and municipal communities across Canada. Instead, our contribution in this book is to provide a generalizable typology and framework that can be applied to any relationship or community in Canada. Our case study chapters demonstrate this fact by classifying and analysing a variety of relationships encompassing a broad range of spatial, demographic, cultural, political, economic, and social contexts.

Chapter Three

Business as Usual: Sault Ste Marie, Garden River, and Batchewana

The intergovernmental relationships between the municipal government of Sault Ste Marie and the band councils of Garden River and Batchewana First Nations in northern Ontario are instances of the business-as-usual partnership type characterized by low levels of institutional interaction (low intensity) and infrequent intercommunity engagement (low engagement). While Sault Ste Marie has concluded numerous agreements with both Indigenous communities, they are all service-delivery arrangements and have not developed into deeper or more institutionalized partnerships. Similarly, communications between the local authorities and Indigenous communities have been characterized by all parties as sporadic and ad hoc, despite some recognition that more interaction could be mutually advantageous.

Our analysis also indicates that most of the factors relating to capacity and willingness have had a negative influence on the development of deeper relationships between the governments. Factors such as institutional asymmetry (institutions), the legacy of previous interactions (history and polarizing events), the entrenchment of powerful personalities and a climate of mistrust based on instances of racism and discrimination (weak community capital) have all acted as barriers to deepening the relationships and expanding cooperation to other policy areas. That there is very little difference in the relationships between Sault Ste Marie and the two Indigenous communities, despite interesting differences in the evolution of those relationships, can be interpreted as a hallmark of the business-as-usual type of relationship – the current leadership of the city regards these agreements largely as transactions that make economic and political sense, in no way different from the

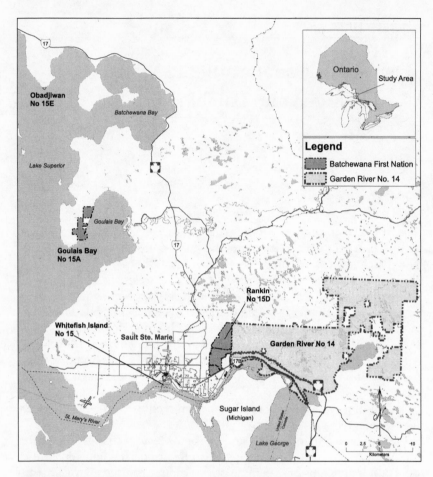

Figure 3.1. Sault Ste Marie, Batchewana First Nation, and Garden River

city's other relationships with neighbouring municipal governments, rather than special or unique partnerships that may serve as a foundation for future governance collaboration (imperative).

Community Profiles

The city of Sault Ste Marie is located on the St Mary's River in northern Ontario, just east of Lake Superior and north of Lake Huron, close to the U.S. border. According to the 2011 census (Statistics Canada 2011b), it has a population of approximately 79,000, and a land base of about 805 square kilometres. National Household Survey Data from 2011 indicate that approximately 9,500 residents identify themselves as Aboriginal, with 7,330 identifying as First Nations, 2,275 as Metis, and 30 as Inuit (Statistics Canada 2011a). The city utilizes a typical municipal government structure. On the political side, a mayor and city council (e.g., twelve councillors representing six wards) exercise executive and legislative functions, with only the conservation authority, the economic development corporation, police, and the public library reporting directly to them. The chief administrative officer oversees the rest of the city bureaucracy, including the clerk's department, community services, engineering and planning, finance, fire and emergency medical services, human resources, legal, public works and transportation, and social services.

Two Indigenous communities are located in close proximity to the city. The first is Garden River First Nation, which is a member of the North Shore Tribal Council and is located just east of Sault Ste Marie, approximately three kilometres away from the city's eastern boundary. The community's land base, which is subject to the 1850 Robinson-Huron Treaty, totals approximately 20,700 hectares. As of March 2013, band membership was 2,665, with approximately 57 per cent of band members living off-reserve. Of those living on-reserve, approximately 30 per cent are under the age of twenty. The band operates under the Indian Act using a band council structure, with twelve councillors and one chief. Approximately 120 people serve in the band's bureaucracy, helping the band council to administer a wide range of services, including police, a bingo hall, a childcare centre, a health-care centre, education and economic development programs, lands and membership, public works, utilities, sports and recreation, housing, and other services. The community has recently developed a comprehensive plan that identifies the community's strengths, weaknesses, and goals and aspirations. The core issues that the community hopes to address are "colonialism and loss of identity, lack of opportunity to learn traditions/teachings, lack of proactive action, [and] dependency on federal government" (Garden River First Nation 2013, 56). Potential remedies include building new and innovative housing, exploring resource protection and new opportunities for economic development, expanding health and wellness programs, strengthening communication and community engagement, and emphasizing teaching and learning (chap. 3).

The second Indigenous community in close proximity to the city of Sault Ste Marie is Batchewana First Nation, which is also a member of the North Shore Tribal Council. This community's reserve lands, which are also subject to the Robinson-Huron Treaty of 1850, include the Rankin Reserve (approximately 1,620 hectares), which is located just east of the city and west of Garden River, the Obadjiwan Reserve (approximately 68 hectares), which is about eighty-five kilometres north of the city, the Goulais Bay Reserve (approximately 645 hectares), which is approximately fifty-six kilometres north of the city, and White-fish Island, which is located just south of the city on the St Mary's River. The Rankin and Whitefish Reserves are closest to the city. According to Aboriginal Affairs and Northern Development Canada (2013) data, the community has a registered population of 2,727, with approximately 800 members living on reserve lands. The band is subject to the Indian Act and operates a conventional chief and council system, with one chief and eight councillors representing the community. The Batchewana government offers a range of programs and services to its members, including language programs, housing, lands and membership, employment and training, economic development, policing, daycare and youth/teen centres, and a bingo/gaming facility.

Agreements and Intergovernmental Issues

The city of Sault Ste Marie has three formal agreements with Garden River First Nation and all are service agreements. The first agreement, which is a fire protection agreement, is no longer in effect (details below) and was signed in 1991.[15] The second agreement, signed in 1996, involves the city taking responsibility for all incoming 9-1-1 calls from Garden River and directing those calls to appropriate emergency services. In exchange, under s. 3.0 of the agreement, the First Nation agrees to provide the city with nine cents per capita per month for the length

---

15 We were unable to obtain a copy of this agreement, but a number of interviewees made us aware of its existence. As well, we are not certain when this agreement was signed. Interviewees, however, have told us that the fire protection agreements with Batchewana and Garden River were completed at the same time. Since the earliest fire protection agreement we have from Batchewana was signed in 1991, we have assumed that the agreement with Garden River was signed in that same year, which is consistent with what interviewees have told us (L. Sayers 2013; Fratesi 2013).

Table 3.1. Garden River Agreements

Agreement	Date	Type	Substance
Fire protection	1991	Service agreement	Sault Ste Marie to provide fire protection in exchange for a fee
Emergency services	1996	Service agreement	Sault Ste Marie to process all 9-1-1 calls from Garden River First Nation
Land lease	2009	Land lease	Agreement for ten-year land lease from Garden River First Nation to Sault Ste Marie to build an ambulance station

of the agreement, which remains in effect. The final agreement, signed in 2009, is a ten-year land-lease agreement in which Garden River First Nation promises to lease a parcel of land to the city so that the city can build an ambulance station to service Laird Hill, the Sylvan Valley Area, Garden River, and the eastern part of Sault Ste Marie (Della-Mattia 2009; Fratesi 2013). Although the city owns and manages the facility, it has staffed it with band members from Garden River and other First Nations (Purvis 2008) (see table 3.1).

In contrast to the few agreements it has with Garden River, the municipal government has many more with Batchewana First Nation. All nine of their agreements are service agreements. Four of the agreements, signed in 1991, 1999, 2004, and 2008, involve the city providing fire protection services on the reserve in accordance with the rules and a fee schedule set out in the agreements. Another agreement, signed in 2007, stipulates that the city will receive and treat a certain amount of sewer discharge from the First Nation once a connection is built between the municipal and First Nation sewage systems. Another agreement, signed in 1990, commits the city to provide water services to the First Nation in return for standard water provision rates. A 1996 agreement involves the city agreeing to handle all incoming 9-1-1 calls from the reserve, similar to the agreement signed with Garden River First Nation. A 1997 agreement establishes the responsibilities of both governments for the winter maintenance of two streets adjacent to their communities. Finally, an agreement signed in 1996 empowers a third party developer to extend a road to connect future residential constructions to both communities (see table 3.2).

Table 3.2. Batchewana Agreements

Agreement	Date	Type	Substance
Water provision	1990	Service agreement	Sault Ste Marie to provide water to Batchewana First Nation for a fee for service
Fire protection	1991 1999 2004 2008	Service agreement	Sault Ste Marie to provide fire protection in exchange for a fee
Emergency services	1996	Service agreement	Sault Ste Marie to process all 9-1-1 calls from Batchewana First Nation
Road maintenance	1997	Service agreement	Establishes the responsibilities for each community for winter road maintenance
Sewer agreement	2007	Service agreement	Sault Ste Marie will receive and treat wastewater from Batchewana First Nation for a fee

All of these formal agreements between the municipal government and the band councils of Garden River and Batchewana deal solely with jurisdictional issues. None of these agreements can be characterized as addressing joint management, capacity building, communication, or decolonization. As a result, we argue that the city's relationships with these First Nations should be classified as low intensity. As well, given that none of the agreements involve or establish frequent and/or regularized interactions between the bands and the municipal government, both sets of relationships with the city have been classified as low engagement.

Beyond these formal agreements, the city of Sault Ste Marie has also had informal discussions with Garden River and Batchewena about a number of issues affecting one or both communities. None of these issues have resulted in any sort of formal or informal agreement. These issues include:

• Planning and development of new municipal subdivisions near the Rankin and Garden River reserves;
• Building of a highway overpass across Garden River and Batchewana lands into the city at Black Road;

- Extending municipal transit services farther into Garden River First Nation;
- Facilitating the private development of a windmill farm in Prince Township;
- Facilitating the private development of the old St Mary's Paper Mill into an Indigenous cultural centre;
- Clearing the way for a developer to build a solar farm on lands near the Rankin Reserve.

As in the formal agreements, the nature of these issues and the discussions surrounding them fall clearly into the jurisdictional-negotiation service-delivery category, rather than the decolonization, capacity-building, joint-management, and relationship-building categories. Similarly, none of these issues have involved frequent or regularized communications. Instead, the discussions have overwhelmingly been infrequent and ad hoc (Amaroso 2013; Corbiere 2013; Fata 2013; Fratesi 2013; McConnell 2013; Nadeau 2013; L. Sayers 2013; Scott 2013). According to city Planning Director Don McConnell (2013), for instance, although he would like to establish a more regularized relationship with his counterparts from both communities, he has had almost no contact with either of them, except in the rare case when a developer has wanted to build a new subdivision close to the two reserves. Similarly, in 2012, Chief Lyle Sayers sent a letter to the mayor asking whether the city would be willing to work with his government to extend municipal transit services onto his reserve (L. Sayers 2013). The city responded by saying that it could not extend a bus route to the reserve because there were areas of the city that needed to be serviced or upgraded first, including the new hospital, the airport, and other parts of the community. Given these other priorities, and the approximate $272,000 price tag for the new bus route, the city rejected Chief Sayers's request (Kelly 2013; Scott 2013; D. Taylor 2013). Since that brief communication, there have been no further discussions about the issue between the two governments, despite continued interest from Garden River officials (L. Sayers 2013).

Given these considerations and the nature of the formal agreements, we argue that the city's relationship with both Indigenous communities should be classified as residing in the lower-right quadrant of table 3.3. Both sets of intergovernmental relations tend to exhibit features of low intensity and engagement; all of the agreements and discussions have focused mainly on service and jurisdictional issues, and all have involved communication patterns that are infrequent and ad hoc, rather

Table 3.3. Sault Ste Marie / Batchewana First Nation / Garden River First Nation Relationship-Type Matrix

Engagement	Intensity	
	High	Low
High	Strong synergy	In the loop
Low	Agreement-centred	Business as usual

than frequent and regularized. What explains these patterns of intergovernmental relations?

Analysis

Our theoretical framework and empirical evidence gathered from the field reveal a variety of factors that seem to have strongly contributed to the emergence of low-intensity and low-engagement relations between these governments. These factors straddle the range of variables outlined in our theoretical framework. This is not to say that cooperation is completely absent between the city and the two First Nations. Indeed, both Indigenous governments have been able to sign jurisdictional negotiation agreements with the municipal government. Yet it is clear from the evidence below that there remain significant obstacles for those actors that have an interest in crafting a more intense and engaged relationship.

Institutions

One barrier to deeper forms of cooperation has been the different decision-making processes for the city and the band councils. Frequently, municipal timelines, which are enshrined in by-laws and provincial statutes, are rigid and short. In the case of planning decisions, for instance, the city has up to 180 days to approve a request from a developer but frequently processes decisions faster than that. The typical review time for the city is six weeks plus 20 days for mandatory consultations. Rarely are Garden River First Nation or Batchewana First Nation able to meet those timelines. According to Planning Director McConnell,

> The City has legally mandated timeframes to work within, and I know they [Batchewana and Garden River] must sometimes think that the time

allowed for consultation is unreasonable. A company bought an old paper mill here, and this would have been two years ago, and they wanted to rezone it, because it was zoned to be a paper mill and they wanted to use it for something else. So we circulated [the proposal] to Batchewana First Nations, because the paper mill is in close proximity to land belonging to Batchewana First Nations. So we sent them all the information, and their response was that we can't respond as an organization within the time frame you've set aside and I appreciate that. Those times frames don't match the amount of time they need to provide a response. (McConnell 2013)

These differences in time frames act as a disincentive for officials interested in Indigenous–local cooperation. If city staff know that band council bureaucrats cannot meet the timelines established by municipal by-laws and provincial legislation, they are less likely to seek or pursue opportunities for high-engagement or high-intensity collaborations.

These observations are similar to ones made by others in different jurisdictions. Fraser and Viswanathan (2013, 13), for instance, have written about the intergovernmental negotiations between the City of Hamilton and neigbouring First Nations, noting, "Scheduling was also pointed to as a roadblock: while municipal planners work according to budgetary schedules, First Nations staff work with different schedules, and have different election calendars. Often municipal planners are eager to achieve goals much quicker than understaffed First Nations planning offices are able." In that same study, another interviewee remarked, "The difference between how First Nations run things and how municipalities run things … further complicates consultation; chiefs take more time to come to decisions, and because of that longer time frame they may lose funding" (14).

Another institutional barrier to cooperation has been a perceived difference in the amount of autonomy that city and band council staff members enjoy. In the case of planning, for instance, city Planning Director McConnell remarked, "I also found, and this may be a perception from my place, is that the people you're dealing with are not the people who have the ability to agree or disagree. It goes to either a committee or it goes to a chief and comes back saying we're OK or we're not OK" (McConnell 2013). When the city receives a land use application that involves city land that is close to the Rankin Reserve, for instance, a person from Batchewana "will read the application and he will call [me] and make sure he understands it ... but that person is not in a position to respond [immediately] on behalf of the tribe even though he may be perfectly capable of doing so" (ibid.). As a result, staff members face powerful disincentives to actively support and pursue projects or relationships that require approval or cooperation from Batchewana and Garden River. It also means that the main responsibility for pursuing cooperation falls to political leaders, which can result in staff members having little motivation or ability to engage in agency and cooperative ventures.

The unique legal status of municipal and band governments has also been a barrier to deeper cooperation. Municipal governments are creatures of provincial legislation and have little to no constitutional authority or leverage. In contrast, band governments are creatures of the federal government through the Indian Act but also have a range of constitutional and legal rights that municipal governments do not have. These rights include Aboriginal rights and title, an inherent right to self-government, and powerful legal obligations in which the Canadian state and third party interests must consult Indigenous communities on issues affecting their lands. These dynamics, it seems, frequently come into play during communication and meetings involving the city and the Indigenous communities by themselves, or in meetings with other levels of government (Corbiere 2013; Nadeau 2013; L. Sayers 2013). According to Joe Fratesi (2013),

> On any given day we are treated differently by our First Nation folks. We are creatures of provincial legislation; we have no authority in the constitution. They treat us as being a different level of government than they are. As you well know, they will argue that they are a separate nation and that their talks should be with the federal government ... They're not equals, they are superior. They have their own direct linkages to the senior levels of government and so they do not have to be part of ours. So again, the relationship is confused at best and it's based on no one ever clearly defining exactly what rights or authority they have in the scheme of things.

Moreover, although it is clear that Indigenous communities have historical injustices they must resolve with the Crown, "we as a municipality have no role to play in that, nor do we have the wherewithal to resolve those issues; but we're in a room being asked to figure out what relationship we could have or would have with them" (ibid.).

A good example of how these legal barriers can affect the propensity and ability to cooperate occurred when the city attempted to purchase approximately six hundred acres of land on the east side of the city near the Rankin Reserve. A developer, Pod Solar (Fratesi 2010), wanted to build a solar farm on these lands, but these properties were provincial Crown lands and managed by the Ontario Realty Corporation. They also were located at the edge of the Rankin Reserve. To acquire and rezone these lands for industrial development, the city had to first purchase them from the province. Before that could happen, the province told the city that it had a duty to consult with Batchewana First Nation, because the proposed lands were adjacent to the Rankin Reserve. This request was problematic, because the city and Batchewana First Nation had very different ideas about what this duty actually meant in practice. The city believed that its "duty to consult" was limited to addressing any reasonable concerns that Batchewana residents near the area might face should the development go forward. Batchewena leaders, however, interpreted the "duty to consult" quite differently, arguing that their consent was necessary before any development could occur (ibid.). After about two years of on-and-off consultations and negotiations, the city eventually gave up and purchased land elsewhere, which the developer eventually used to build his solar farm (Fratesi 2013).

In some ways, these events and experiences are somewhat unsurprising. Abele et al. (2011), for instance, have found that municipal officials in Thunder Bay and Toronto "were puzzled by the very notion of 'urban Aboriginal policy.'" According to one Toronto official, "'The City of Toronto has no jurisdiction and/or requirement in this area' (Interview 6)." These experiences and perspective are also consistent with Ryan Walker's (2008) arguments about the need to improve the "municipal–Aboriginal" interface. Although municipal governments are aware of the need to incorporate Indigenous peoples into local planning, any efforts to do so will fail unless non-Aboriginal actors properly recognize the role of Aboriginal rights and "community aspirations for meaningful measures of self-determination" (24). Until Sault Ste Marie officials recognize the history and legacies of colonialism and their legal duties to consult, cooperation will remain difficult and most likely limited to business-type transactions (Wood 2003, 467; Fraser and Viswanathan 2013, 11; Belanger and Walker 2009).

Resources

Although differences in resources among actors can sometimes play a significant role in determining whether cooperation occurs, we did not find any significant resource issues in this set of case studies. There was some limited mention of capacity barriers and the negative impact of staff turnover on cooperation, but for the most part, resource issues did not seem to play a significant role in the negotiations and agreements. We did find one issue, but only one, that turned on the availability of funds (or lack thereof) to pay for services; this issue involved the request for a new bus route into Garden River First Nation, which fundamentally came down to, at least for the city, whether an additional $272,000 could be found to pay for the route. Neither the city nor the First Nation was willing to pay that sum yearly, so that issue has remained unresolved.

In terms of staff turnover, one interviewee mentioned that he had cultivated a relationship with his counterpart at one of the First Nations, which for a short time led to regular informal meetings about once a year either in person or at the yearly meetings organized by the Ontario Professional Planners Institute. However, once that band official was moved to another department, that relationship disappeared. As McConnell put it,

> I know Batchewana had a fellow by the name of James Roach who we were dealing with and he was excellent, but they put him in charge of a different operation. The new fellow they brought in was actually an older gentleman who is a really cooperative and good guy, but again we don't work with each other enough ... They're not sure who I am and I'm not sure who they are ... so they're not comfortable because they don't really know who I am ... We don't have that [sense of comfort] with either Garden River or Batchewana. It's not their fault; it's just that we don't have a lot of contact. (McConnell, 2013)

On the issue of capacity, the only issue identified was some differences in policies and information management systems, which can make cooperation difficult. For instance, in the area of social services, the city and First Nation data systems are incompatible and "so when someone moves from Batchewana [to Sault Ste Marie], which is two kilometres away, we have to start all over again and find out the client history. It's like starting from scratch," when it does not have to be that way (Nadeau 2013). There has been some talk among some First Nations in Ontario about adopting a more compatible data management system, but nothing has happened yet.

External Intervention

Another barrier to deeper cooperation has been the actions of the provincial government. In November 2007, the Ontario government opened a new section of the Trans-Canada Highway (Highway 17), which ran north of and around the communities of Echo Bay and through Garden River First Nation. The construction of this bypass required the province to negotiate with Garden River First Nation because the bypass ran through its lands. The original plan was to run the bypass through to the northeast part of Sault Ste Marie up to Black Road. However, this plan never came to fruition because the province was unable to negotiate with Batchewana First Nation to run the bypass through its lands. As a result, the province instead connected the new bypass back to the old Highway 17B at Trunk Road, much to the chagrin of city officials because the current highway does not provide an interchange into the city (see figure 3.2). Had the new bypass run through Batchewana lands and then connected at Black Road, an interchange could have been built, bringing much-needed traffic to the area (Corbiere 2013; Fata 2013; McConnell 2013). It also may have reduced the likelihood of truck-related accidents on the highway; the existing bypass contains a series of sharp and awkward turns, which would not have existed had the bypass been constructed on Batchewana lands (Amaroso 2013).

The failure of the province to negotiate successfully and simultaneously with both Indigenous communities has created some negative feelings among city officials towards Batchewana First Nation. According to one municipal official, "There is another irritation that we have; it's with Batchewana, the highway bypass ... As soon as it [the new highway] hit the boundary of Garden River and Rankin, the project stopped and they had to divert back to the original highway because they couldn't make a similar deal with the Batchewana band ... So for 0.6 of a mile or kilometre, I'm not sure, Rankin has been holding up the completion of the bypass. So that was 11 million dollars spent needlessly as far as I'm concerned" (Fratesi 2013).

Some interviewees blame the province for failing to negotiate with both Indigenous communities at the same time. They claim that the province negotiated with Garden River first, and then Batchewana, and

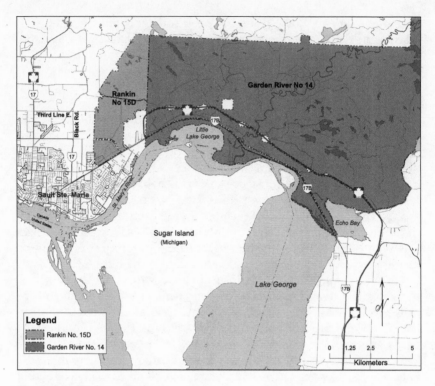

Figure 3.2. Highway Bypass

that it was not willing to offer the same type of compensation that it offered to Garden River. Regardless of the reasons, the key point for this study is that the failure of the province (e.g., external intervention) to negotiate agreements with the two Indigenous groups resulted in a highway bypass that was unacceptable to the city. This in turn has generated some negative feelings, at least among some high-level officials in the city, towards Batchewana First Nation for not providing consent for the original bypass plan.

History and Polarizing Events

Although minor events have contributed both positively (e.g., Garden River's decision to work with the province to build the highway overpass) and negatively (e.g., Batchewana's refusal to agree to either the

land purchase for the solar farm or the extension of the highway overpass through its land), only one polarizing event seems to have had
a strong and lasting impact on the city's relationship with one of its
neighbouring First Nations. In 1991, the municipal government negotiated and signed fire-protection service agreements with both Indigenous communities. Under the terms of the agreements, remuneration
was based on a complex formula that took into account the size of the
on-reserve population, per capita costs, and a number of other factors. Sometime after the agreements went into effect, the city moved
to adjust the remuneration rate. Batchewana First Nation agreed to the
adjustment but Garden River First Nation, after considering the request
for a year, ultimately rejected the new rate and decided to create its
own fire department. The city responded by sending them a bill for
approximately $65,000 for the fire protection services that it claimed
it had provided to the band (Fratesi 2010, 2013). Garden River First
Nation refused to pay that bill because when it signed the agreement in
1991, it did not know that the federal Department of Indian Affairs and
Northern Development (DIAND) was providing the city with funds to
subsidize the cost of providing fire-protection services to the reserve.
Upon learning that the DIAND was providing these funds, Garden
River decided to opt out of its agreement with the city so that it could
receive those funds directly to create its own fire department. As such,
Garden River leaders maintain that that their community does not owe
the city anything (Fratesi 2013; L. Sayers 2013).

Despite this polarizing event occurring almost twenty-five years ago,
some senior leaders in the city and in Garden River continue to see it as
a looming shadow over their relationships with each other. Chief Lyle
Sayers (2013) notes, "At the time, Joe Fratesi was the mayor and shortly
after he became the CAO, and he has been a thorn in our side. Every
time we brought up fire protection or anything else, he would bring that
up – that we owed him money. We didn't owe him anything. So that's a
part of it between our councils and that particular relationship over the
years." Similarly, Fratesi (2013) notes,

There is an outstanding bill that maybe we shouldn't remember, but in
any dealings we have with them, at the back of our mind, we have that
unpaid bill that they were very cavalier about ... and that is not the way
that any neighbour should deal with another neighbour. So back to your
question, we do business regularly with one because of the good relationship that we've had in the past. We don't do business with the other for a

couple of reasons: one is our past history with them and second they have asked us to provide services but they aren't prepared to pay for it on a cost-recovery basis and that's not fair to the taxpayers of Sault Ste Marie.

Imperative

In terms of imperatives for cooperation, the issues that have emerged have been fairly low level. The Indigenous communities seem to be interested in service agreements with the city, at least for those services that they cannot reasonably afford to deliver on their own (Kelly 2013; Purvis 2008; D. Taylor 2013), and the municipality is happy to provide those services as long as the band councils are willing and able to pay for them. In terms of the bus route, for instance, "It has been suggested by [Sault Ste Marie] Transit Services the First Nation start its own transit service and link up passengers with the City of Sault Ste Marie's Riverside bus route at the corner of Trunk and Fournier Roads. Sayers says Garden River has looked for funding from the federal government to start up its own transit service, but has been told 'There are other priorities'" (D. Taylor 2013), so Garden River approached the city about providing this service.

Similarly, and more broadly, according to Joe Fratesi (2013), "We have service agreements with them [Garden River and Batchewana] and we have service agreements with other neighbouring jurisdictions who are not First Nation and we don't have regular meetings with them. If we have a service that we can provide, and they are prepared to pay for those services, and we can conveniently extend them, then we offer it to them … [but] unless there is a need, we don't have communication with the township of Prince [or the First Nations]." Nicholas Apostle (2013), Sault Ste Marie commissioner of community services, agrees with the general thrust of this comment, stating that within his domain of responsibility, "there have not been any real [parks and recreation] issues to look at or talk about in a regular reoccurring meeting. Just on a case-by-case [basis], but that seems to have worked."

In short, none of the issues that have arisen so far have been high-level or high-intensive priorities for either community. None of the communities have expressed any strong or powerful need or desire for deeper forms of intergovernmental partnership. In the case of the third party request to build a solar farm, neither Batchewana nor the city faced strong incentives to agree to the sale of the land, especially when the developer was willing to build his solar farm elsewhere. In the case of the bus route, Garden River does have a bus service that leads to the border of its reserve, meaning that residents do have access to a bus service, albeit one that is inconvenient for Garden River residents. The highway overpass, while somewhat important to the city, was not an issue that involved direct negotiations between the city and First Nations. Instead, it was a negotiation between the province and the First Nations, with implications for the city. Although there is continued interest from the city and Batchewana to eventually complete the highway bypass (Amaroso 2013; Corbiere 2013; Fata 2013; McConnell 2013), none of the interviewees believe that the issue is pressing.

The future, however, may be different as Garden River begins implementing its new community plan (P. Sayers 2013). One band plan is to supplement its golf course by building a new hotel and conference centre. These new ventures could have a negative impact on the city by drawing business away from Sault Ste Marie. At the time the fieldwork was conducted, the band had yet to communicate its intentions to the city, although it intended to do so within a couple of weeks once it had finalized its plans (L. Sayers 2013). In other words, as both First Nations ramp up their plans for economic development, these plans may have significant positive or negative implications for the city, which may create stronger imperatives for deeper forms of cooperation.

Community Capital

One core feature of community capital is the extent to which the communities interact with each other day to day. Many of our interviewees noted that members from both Indigenous communities are frequent visitors to the city, whether to work, attend school, play hockey, go shopping, or engage in other activities. Former Buffalo Sabres Head Coach Ted Nolan, for instance, is a member of Garden River and for the longest time was head coach of the Sault Ste Marie Greyhounds. In recognition of his work, he was awarded the city's highest honour, even though he was a resident and member of Garden River. Moreover, there is some cooperation among businesses and community leaders, especially on cultural and other civic events (Apostle 2013; P. Sayers 2013). So at first blush, there seems to be a lot of positive intercommunity interaction between the city and Indigenous members from

Batchewana and Garden River. Yet, at the same time, while "people are transient from the community [in terms of] coming into the city, there's not a lot of information going on between the First Nation and the city on both sides ... First Nations are very protective of their data and information. You know, there's a lack of trust there, and that lack of trust hinders information coming across, and so I just think that there's a lot of work to do to strengthen that relationship" (Nadeau 2013).

More importantly, another recurrent theme from the interview data is the perceived existence of cultural racism in the city (L. Sayers 2013). Joseph Corbiere (2013), for instance, mentioned how his opinion pieces in the local newspaper regularly draw commentators from the city that are extremely hostile and offensive to Indigenous rights and issues. He also told us several stories about racist comments towards Indigenous students that were made by Sault Ste Marie volunteers and education leaders in other forums. Indeed, one of the first comments from one of the interviewees was that racism was a major barrier to cooperation with city officials. According to Lyle Sayers (2013), "Not everybody is a racist. I'm not brushing everybody in town with that brush, but when it comes down to the nitty-gritty, we're left out of everything. Even the bidding process, they tried to stop us a couple of years ago ... They don't want to share anything. But if you look at it from our end, every-thing we do the city has benefited from. They probably say that we get along because we don't bitch. We don't complain. We do our stuff and they do their stuff. So really, we're not doing anything [in terms of cooperative efforts]."

These perceptions of racism are confirmed by a 2004 report that analysed 239 survey responses and thirteen in-depth interviews with residents of Sault Ste Marie. Some of the main findings of that report include:

- "A majority of respondents, 53.5%, said they have observed dis-crimination based on race against someone in Sault Ste Marie in the past year" (Curry 2004, 24).
- "Stores and restaurants were the dominant location where discrimi-nation based on race occurred, with 21 whites and 34 racialized minorities witnessing it occurring there" (Curry 2004, 27).
- "More than half of the aboriginals, 52.2%, said they personally were discriminated against because of their race in the city in the past year" (Curry 2004, 30).

Typical comments from the in-depth interviews included:

- "I hear things that are negative about aboriginals all the time, especially at work (in a bar). White female questionnaire respondent" (Curry 2004, 25).
- "Teachers centre out our kids against non-native kids. A waitress or store clerk takes someone else's order before us. Clerks speak rudely to you but the next person who comes in is non-Indian and their voice and attitude changes. Hockey rink parents make comments about native kids on the ice or make gestures. Nurses are ignorant and speak to our people as if they are children. Native female questionnaire respondent" (Curry 2004, 25).
- "I was next in line at a coffee shop and they asked the person behind me what he wanted, so I walked out. Native male questionnaire respondent" (Curry 2004, 28).

In short, these data suggest that there indeed seems to be a culture of racism in Sault Ste Marie, which in turn seems to have had a negative impact on the willingness of Indigenous political leaders and others to seek out cooperative relationships (Corbiere 2013; L. Sayers 2013).

As has already been alluded to above, political leadership has also been a barrier to the emergence of more intensive and engaged cooperation between the municipal government and both Indigenous communities. Although city councillors and mayors have been interested in pursuing more cooperative relations over the years (Amaroso 2013; Corbiere 2013; Fata 2013), the relationships of a number of other, more entrenched leaders with each other have proven to be an obstacle for some time. As is clear from examples above, one particularly problematic relationship has been between Indigenous leaders and former Sault Ste Marie mayor (1986–96), and now chief administrative officer (1996–present), Joe Fratesi. Despite the election of new mayors such as John Rowsell (2006–10) (Fata 2013), and the current mayor, Debbie Amaroso, Fratesi's presence at the top of the city's civil service seems to continue to be somewhat problematic, though by no means insurmountable (L. Sayers 2013). Yet officials from both Indigenous communities have mentioned that Fratesi has sometimes made it difficult for them to pursue more intense and frequent cooperation.

Overall, although we have classified the city's relationships with both neighbouring band councils as characterized by low intensity and low engagement, we should also note that there were small differences between Batchewana's and Garden River's relationships with the city. The most notable difference was the higher number of agreements signed by Batchewana versus those signed by Garden River. This numerical difference is probably the result of history, polarizing events, and leadership effects related to Garden River's allegedly unpaid fire-protection bill for services rendered in the early 1990s. Yet we do not think that this difference detracts from our classification, for two reasons. First, although Batchewana has signed more agreements with the city compared to Garden River, all of its agreements are service agreements; and, despite these agreements, we have yet to see the emergence of frequent or regularized communication. Second, although Garden River has fewer agreements with the city, it still has been able to engage in more recent yet still highly infrequent dialogue with the city, including signing a land-lease agreement to build an ambulance station on the reserve. Although this agreement may one day improve the relationship between the city and Garden River, relations continue to be characterized by low levels of intensity and engagement.

Conclusion

This chapter presented some evidence that the city of Sault Ste Marie enjoys a "business as usual" relationship with the Garden River and Batchewana First Nations. More specifically, our analysis of the data suggests that the capacity and willingness of both sets of actors to cooperate generated a distinctive set of relationships characterized by low engagement and low intensity. In particular, cooperation seems to have been driven by low-level, service delivery-related interests, rather than high-priority issues and motivations. Perceptions of racism and a history of (mildly) contentious interactions also affected actors' willingness to engage more deeply, particularly in the face of resource constraints and a lack of mutually beneficial imperatives that addressed issues beyond the provision of municipal services. At the same time, factors relating to capacity also made it difficult for the communities to move beyond these low levels of engagement and intensity. Given these findings, we anticipate that the nature and intensity of these relationships are unlikely to change in the near future.

Chapter Four

Strong Synergy: Village of Teslin and Teslin Tlingit Council

In this chapter, we focus on and examine the intergovernmental relationship between the Teslin Tlingit Council (TTC) and the Village of Teslin (VOT), both of which are located in Yukon Territory (see figure 4.1). Much like the previous chapter, we begin by describing the two communities, the formal agreements that they have signed with each other, and some of the current and ongoing issues under discussion. We then classify and explain this intergovernmental relationship using our analytical framework and typology. Our findings suggest that the VOT and the TTC have developed a very different relationship compared to what we found in the Sault Ste Marie region. Whereas in the previous chapter the relationships between Indigenous and local authorities were characterized by low engagement and low intensity, the Village of Teslin and the Tlingit Council have a strong synergy relationship characterized by frequent interactions and highly institutionalized cooperation.

In contrast to the Sault Ste Marie relationships, most of the framework factors in this case stimulated cooperation and deeper relationships between communities. For example, the treaty status of TTC communities created a powerful actor with whom the weaker Village of Teslin saw many benefits in partnering, with the result that institutional asymmetries (institutions) were a foundation rather than a barrier to cooperation. Very strong community integration and cross-appointment of leadership between the two governments (community capital) contributed to the further deepening of the relationship. This integration has created a shared vision of the region and how each community can leverage its advantages to the collective benefit. It has also contributed to an environment in which communities can see beyond their own narrow interests and are willing to partner on projects with

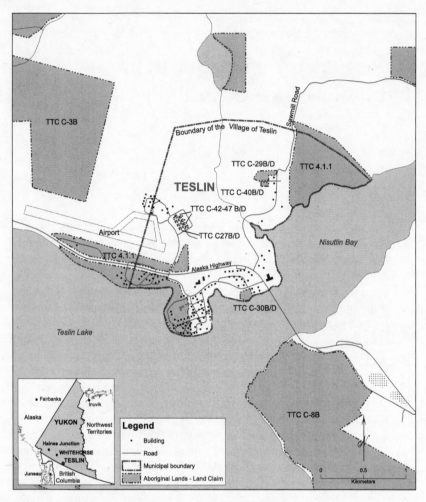

Figure 4.1. Village of Teslin and Teslin Tlingit Council

uneven distributions of costs and/or benefits in the recognition that the entire region will benefit.

While it may be tempting to interpret the outcomes in this case and other strong synergy cases more generally as superior to the business-as-usual arrangements because of the strength and potential of these relationships, it is important to assess them both equally. Both relationship types have resulted in cooperation that purportedly fulfils the needs of the communities involved. As such, they are both successful relationships in their own ways. The Village of Teslin and the TTC are also much smaller communities located in very close proximity to one another, which may accord some advantages in the development of community capital that were weaker in Sault Ste Marie. What is most significant about the contrast in experiences between the most and least integrated and engaged cases is that similar factors play very different roles (e.g., institutions) in encouraging or discouraging cooperation. However, in both cases community capital, and its impact on willingness to engage in cooperative relationships, played the most significant role in shaping inter-community relations.

Community Profiles

The Village of Teslin, Yukon Territory, is located approximately 183 kilometres east of Whitehorse on the Alaska Highway (at kilometre marker 1244), nestled between Teslin Lake and Nisutlin Bay. According to the 2011 census (Statistics Canada 2012), the community has a population of 122 and a land base of 1.92 square kilometres. The Village of Teslin website (Village of Teslin 2014) suggests that the community actually has about 450 residents, of whom 300 are Teslin Tlingit citizens. The city utilizes a typical municipal government structure. On the political side, a mayor and three councillors exercise executive and legislative functions, while a chief administrative officer oversees the village's bureaucracy and public servants (which include a treasurer, a public works foreman, a recreation programmer, an administrative assistant, and members of a volunteer fire department). The community has a number of recreational facilities, including a baseball diamond, a skateboard park, a friendship park, and a recreation complex (which houses an arena, a small bar, and other amenities). There is also a museum in the area, as well as the Teslin Tlingit Heritage Centre, a grocery store, two motels, a resort, and a campground. There are also a variety of other small businesses in the area (ibid.; Village of Teslin and Teslin Tlingit Council 2009, 13).

Immediately adjacent to but also partly within the Village of Teslin are the traditional territories of the Teslin Tlingit people. According to its website (Teslin Tlingit Council 2014b), the Teslin Tlingit community has approximately 800 citizens; 300 of these citizens live in and around the Village of Teslin and another 200 live in Whitehorse. The Teslin Tlingit are a self-governing Indigenous group, having completed a comprehensive land claims agreement and a self-government agreement in 1995. These agreements put into practice and modify many of the general provisions set out in the 1994 Umbrella Final Agreement (UFA), which was negotiated and ratified in March 1993 by the Council of Yukon Indians on behalf of all fourteen Yukon First Nations in the territory (Alcantara 2013, 86–7).

The Teslin Tlingit community was the first of an initial group of four Yukon First Nations to complete an individual final agreement in 1995. Under the terms of its land claims agreement (Teslin Tlingit Council 1993a), the community received title and jurisdiction to over 1,230 square kilometres of Category A land (surface and subsurface title), 1,165 square kilometres of Category B land (surface title only), and 33.36 square kilometres of reserve lands. Although the community has parcels of settlement land throughout its traditional territory, TTC citizens in the area reside almost exclusively on settlement lands within the Village of Teslin and the Foxpoint subdivision, which is just 4 kilometres outside the municipal boundary (Wirth 2014). In addition to land ownership rights, the Teslin Tlingit received $21,646,715 to be paid over fifteen years, as well as a range of rights and responsibilities over economic development, fish and wildlife, special management areas (e.g., the Nisutlin River Delta National Wildlife Area), heritage, and other land-related issues. Under its self-government agreement (Teslin Tlingit Council 1993b, 16–18), the Teslin Tlingit also secured a comprehensive range of governance-related subject matters. Some of these jurisdictions include health care, education, social and welfare services, training programs, childcare, inheritance and wills, the administration of justice, the solemnization of marriage, the use and management of settlement lands, transportation, and taxation. Much like other self-government agreements, the TTC determines the exact timing and nature of how it will exercise authority over these areas.

To put these new powers and responsibilities into practice, the Teslin Tlingit community drafted and ratified a formal and written constitution. This foundational document lays out the structure, organization, and public administration of the Teslin Tlingit's new government, called the Teslin Tlingit Council (TTC), as well as a number of rules governing citizenship enrolment, leadership selection, elections, and the management of public revenues, expenditures, and assets, among other things (Teslin Tlingit Council 2013). Generally speaking, the TTC operates under an Aboriginal self-government model (see Alcantara and Wilson 2014; Henderson 2008) rather than the more well-known public (e.g., government of Nunavut) or more frequently used Indian Act models (Alcantara and Whitfield 2010; Henderson 2008).

Fundamental to the organizational logic of the TTC is the traditional clan structure of the community. The five clans of the TTC are Kùkh-hittàn (Raven Child Clan), Ishkìtàn (Frog Clan), Yanyèdi (Wolf Clan), Dèshitàn (Beaver Clan), and Dakhl'awèdi (Eagle Clan). Each clan has a leader (as specified and named in the constitution) and a number of elders, and they organize themselves and choose their members according to their own customs and traditions (Teslin Tlingit Council 2014b).

The formal structure of the TTC government revolves around four different councils, each of which exercises executive, legislative, and/or administrative functions. The nine-member Executive Council, which is made up of the chief executive officer (CEO), the deputy chief, a youth councillor, the executive elder, and one councillor from each clan, initiates and oversees the administration and enforcement of all laws, regulations, and policies passed by the General Council. Executive Council members (with the exception of the executive elder) generally serve four-year terms and are selected by their appropriate council or clan (e.g., the CEO and deputy chief are chosen by the General Council; clan representatives are chosen through the General Council by their individual clans, etc.). The twenty-five-member General Council, which is made up of five representatives serving four-year terms and appointed by each of the five clans, exercises the legislative power (e.g., pass laws, review budgets, amend the constitution) within the TTC and serves as the main authority to which all other councils and bodies report. The Elders Council is an advisory body made up of all Teslin Tlingit elders aged sixty-five years or older. It provides direction and knowledge to all of the other bodies and departments in the TTC government. Finally, the Justice Council, which is composed of one member representing and appointed by each clan (for a total of five members), oversees the implementation of the 2011 Administration of Justice Agreement, which allows the TTC to "impose penalties for violations of TTC laws; appoint individuals to enforce and prosecute violations of these laws; and, establish a Peacemaker Court to adjudicate violations and to reconsider decisions made by TTC government officials or administrative bodies" (Teslin Tlingit Council 2014b). In addition to these councils, the TTC also employs a Management Board that serves as the main coordinating body for the TTC's bureaucracy, which itself includes a range of departments such as Finance and Administration, Health and Social Development, Lands and Resources, Capital and Infrastructure,

Negotiations and Implementation, Justice, Heritage, and Workforce Development (ibid.).

Existing Agreements and Intergovernmental Issues

The VOT and TTC have signed five formal agreements over the last ten years (see table 4.1). Two of the agreements address relationship building (e.g., a memorandum of understanding [MOU] and an Integrated Community Sustainability Plan), and three of them focus on the joint management of newly built infrastructure, programs, and services. All five of these agreements are noteworthy because they involve relatively high levels of engagement and intense interactions between the governments.

The first formal agreement successfully negotiated by the VOT and the TTC was an Infrastructure and Services Memorandum of Understanding, signed in July 2005. Described as a "political accord" rather than a legal one (Village of Teslin and Teslin Tlingit Council 2005a, 4), this MOU states that the parties recognize "the fundamental importance of mutually beneficial relations" and "wish to facilitate evolving inter-governmental relationships" with each other (1–2). This includes maintaining a "regular dialogue with the continuation of the monthly meetings (currently the Village Council and the TTC Executive Council meet the first Monday of each month) and where relevant the promotion of meetings of officials of each party on specific matters" (3). It also means working "cooperatively in conducting discussions and negotiations with other [levels of] governments on matters within the scope of this MOU." Section 2 of the document states that the governments will seriously consider forming a regional administrative and planning structure to streamline existing regulations and decision-making. Finally, the document states that they will work together to ensure that members from both communities "receive a high level of service delivered at cost effective pricing" (1). To do so, they will negotiate a set of separate agreements to address "the orderly provision of governmental services to TTC Settlement Land parcels, lands within VOT boundaries and the surrounding area, including without limitation ... sewage system upgrades and maintenance; recreational facilities (upgrading, construction and maintenance); waste system upgrades and maintenance; roads; solid waste management; and economic development," among other things (2). In short, this MOU is very much a relationship-building agreement because it recognizes and creates new spaces for

Table 4.1. Village of Teslin / Teslin Tlingit Council Agreements

Agreement	Date	Type	Substance
Infrastructure and Services Memorandum of Understanding	2005	Relationship building	To foster dialogue between the governments on a range of issues
Teslin Sewer Development Agreement	2005	Joint management	To facilitate construction of a new sewer line
Skateboard Park Agreement	2005	Joint management	To build a new skateboard park on VOT lands
Teslin Integrated Community Sustainability Plan	2007	Relationship building	A joint vision to create a healthy and sustainable community of Teslin
Recreation Contribution Agreement	2011	Joint management	To create a new recreational program and recreational programmer position to serve both communities

regularized dialogue, collaboration, and cooperation, including the possibility of forming a new regional/district governance structure to coordinate policymaking.

Several months later, the VOT and the TTC completed two additional agreements in September and December 2005, respectively. Both are of the joint-management variety. The first agreement was the Teslin Sewer Development Agreement, signed on 1 September 2005. Previous to this agreement, municipal sewage was transported by truck to a nearby sewage lagoon, which was inefficient, costly, and potentially hazardous to the environment. To mitigate these concerns, the VOT secured approximately $2 million in federal and territorial funding to build a new sewer line from VOT lands to a nearby sewage lagoon. The most direct path for this new line was through TTC lands and so VOT sought and successfully negotiated an intergovernmental agreement with TTC (Wirth 2014). Under the terms of this agreement, VOT agreed to:

- consult TTC on the design and appearance of any new buildings involved in the project;
- seek an easement from TTC in accordance with TTC laws;
- appoint a TTC representative to serve on the sewer line project management team for the duration of the construction; and

- provide TTC with future access to the line at no additional cost should TTC decide that it wanted to connect part of its settlement lands to the new line (Village of Teslin and Teslin Tlingit Council 2005c).

In short, this document is a joint-management agreement rather than a typical fee-for-service arrangement.

The second joint-management agreement, signed in December 2005, was a Skateboard Park Agreement. Under the terms of this arrangement, the TTC agreed to build a skateboarding park on VOT lands near the arena in the village square (Wirth 2014). In exchange, the VOT provided TTC with $25,000 to offset construction costs associated with the project. Custodial and cleaning services for the park would be provided by the VOT, and both governments would jointly undertake ongoing repairs and maintenance of the facilities once they were completed. The agreement also stipulated that although the Teslin Recreational Society, a non-governmental organization, was not a signatory, it "has purchased equipment suitable for a skate board park" and will provide that equipment to TTC for installation (Village of Teslin and Teslin Tlingit Council 2005b, 1). This agreement, in short, is a joint-management partnership because of the intensity and level of intergovernmental interactions mandated by the document.

In 2007, the governments signed a fourth formal agreement, called the Teslin Integrated Community Sustainability Plan (ICSP). This agreement, which was revised in 2009, emerged out of planning initiated by the VOT in early 2006. Initially, the VOT intended to create its own ICSP but very quickly decided to work with the TTC to form a joint planning committee and draft "one common plan for the whole community of Teslin" (Village of Teslin and Teslin Tlingit Council 2009, 3). Much like other ICSPs found in other parts of the country, Teslin's plan outlined a short-, medium-, and long-term vision for the community. It declared that both communities would work together to provide "for the long term social, cultural and economic needs of its residents while protecting and respecting the natural environment that sustains them" (6). To achieve this vision, the document identified community values and goals, which include:

- "Respect for our neighbours, our community and ourselves ...
- The health of our residents ...
- Knowledge, learning, and education ...

- Our Tlingit heritage and culture …
- The natural environment that sustains our community …
- A diverse and sustainable economy" (6–9).

The plan then assessed the challenges, successes, and failures of the community with respect to each of these goals and values before describing and assessing a number of focus areas, including water, transportation, energy, solid waste, and a variety of short to long-term infrastructure priorities. The document concluded by identifying a range of issues and concerns that could be mitigated through the signing of future service provision agreements between the two governments (Village of Teslin and Teslin Tlingit Council 2009, 1).

The Teslin ICSP is a remarkable document because it represents a joint commitment to create one, unified, sustainable, and healthy community. Rather than the VOT and the TTC developing their own ICSPs, as other municipalities and First Nations have done in Canada (see Moore, Walker, and Skelton 2011, 36), these governments decided to create a joint plan, which speaks to their strong interest in fostering closer links with each other (Wirth 2014). As such, and in many ways, the Teslin ICSP is an excellent example of a relationship-building agreement. It emerged out of a joint planning process between the TTC Executive Council and the VOT municipal council and involved interviews with community stakeholders, public presentations, input gathering from schools and youth, reviews of planning documents from both communities, and hosting public meetings in March and October 2007 (Village of Teslin and Teslin Tlingit Council, 2009, 3–4). The result was a document to guide not only the intergovernmental relationship between the two governments, but also the construction of a sustainable and healthy community of Teslin.

The final formal agreement signed by the TTC and the VOT was a Recreation Contribution Agreement, completed in November 2011. This arrangement evolved from discussions in 2006 and 2007 between the communities on the installation of artificial ice in the arena. At the time, the VOT agreed to fully fund and install the artificial ice in exchange for the TTC helping with ongoing costs. Out of that informal arrangement, the two governments negotiated a much larger recreation contribution partnership (Wirth 2014). Under the terms of that agreement, the TTC agreed to provide the VOT with $25,000 a year to fund VOT recreation programming and $40,000 a year to hire a recreation programmer to be supervised by VOT staff. In exchange, the VOT agreed to match these financial contributions, keep track of and report on the spending of these funds, include the TTC in the recruitment of the recreation programmer, and work with the TTC to develop programming relevant for the entire Teslin community (Village of Teslin and Teslin Tlingit Council 2011, 1–2). Much like two of the previous agreements discussed above, this agreement is a joint-management partnership involving a much more entangled relationship than the typical municipal service provision arrangement. Both communities sacrificed autonomy in the form of money and control to jointly create a new recreation program and a recreation programmer position; the programmer was hired and funded by both communities but placed under the administrative authority of the VOT.

The nature and content of these five formal agreements suggest that the VOT and the TTC share an intergovernmental relationship that is characterized by relatively high levels of engagement and intensity. The 2005 MOU provided a solid foundation for the negotiation of future agreements. It also affirmed that the parties would continue holding regular meetings with each other to discuss common issues (see also Curran 2014). The 2007 Teslin ICSP committed the communities to work closely together towards the creation of a unified, healthy, and sustainable Teslin community. It did so by providing a comprehensive plan for a variety of short-, medium-, and long-term priorities, problems, and opportunities common to both communities. The remaining three formal agreements were joint-management agreements whose provisions and terms went far beyond what is typically found in most municipal service provision agreements. In particular, these agreements encouraged significant interaction between the governments, including regular consultation, communication, input, and even joint management of building the new sewer line, the skateboard park, and community recreational programming. The governments ceded significant autonomy in exchange for the production of collective and public goods, especially compared to the agreements and relationships surveyed in the previous chapter. In short, these five formal agreements represent a highly engaged and intense intergovernmental relationship between one municipality and its neighbouring First Nation in Yukon Territory.

Of course, formal agreements are only part of the story. The VOT and the TTC have a number of informal agreements and ongoing issues that they are currently navigating and negotiating with each other. In the informal arrangements between these governments, the VOT provides a number of municipal services to TTC lands on a fee-for-service, cost-recovery basis. These services include fire protection, water delivery and wastewater, and solid-waste management (Across the River Consulting and Urban Systems 2013, 8). For TTC properties within municipal boundaries, for instance, the VOT charges "$0.0095 per litre (monthly min of $25)" for water, and $20 and $45 a month for residential and commercial solid-waste removal, respectively. For TTC properties outside municipal boundaries, it charges an extra $10 for water delivery; otherwise its water and solid-waste rates are exactly the same as they charge for these services within municipal boundaries (ibid.). Each government maintains its own roads and street lighting, although occasionally the TTC will hire the VOT to steam its culverts in exchange for a standard hourly rate. Fire protection services are provided to the TTC free of charge. Finally, the TTC owns and maintains a community cemetery, which it allows any and all citizens from either community to use at no additional cost. Overall, these informal arrangements are characterized by mostly low-level engagement and intensity interactions between the governments, usually using a fee-for-service or no charge model, depending on the service being provided.

Finally, in ongoing negotiations, the VOT and the TTC are discussing two issues that have evolved out of, and are consistent with, their MOU and ICSP: municipal boundary expansion and negotiation of a comprehensive servicing agreement. Recently, the Village of Teslin undertook a study to explore the possibility of "filing a proposal with the Yukon Municipal Board to expand the boundaries of the municipality. The objective is to provide for a more cohesive community and the most efficient and cost effective service delivery" for TTC and VOT residents (Across the River Consulting and Urban Systems 2013, 1), two objectives that are explicitly mentioned in the 2005 MOU and the 2007 Teslin ICSP. Other reasons for pursuing a municipal boundary expansion include "enfranchising the currently peripheral population for Village elections and allowing for a dense, more efficient and affordable new Sawmill Road subdivision ... However, the primary benefits could be greater local property tax revenues and improved services" (25). According to the study, the impact of the proposal should be, on the whole, slightly positive for the entire region, with the VOT gaining and the TTC losing some revenues:

Extending the Village's boundary would appear to have limited impact on service levels. Those properties that would be brought into the Village under the proposed boundary expansion already receive a comprehensive suite of services from the Village. The most significant change in the level of service would be the increase in water delivery from once a week to three times a week. The most significant change in service responsibility could be for the roads on TTC lands e.g. Foxpoint Subdivision.

In total, the Village is expected to experience a gain of $54,590 if the boundary is expanded as proposed. TTC is expected to experience a loss of $22,702. TTC citizens would gain $6,585.

There is a notable net positive impact to the local community as a whole of $46,334 as tax levies are redirected from Government of Yukon to Village of Teslin. (ibid.)

The two communities continue to discuss the possibility of boundary expansion but have yet to sign or reach an agreement on the issue.

A second item under discussion between the two communities, which is related to the municipal boundary expansion proposal, is the negotiation of a comprehensive servicing agreement. Currently, as mentioned above, the VOT provides municipal services to TTC lands on an informal, fee-for-service, cost-recovery, and ad hoc basis. The two governments are exploring the possibility of formalizing and modifying those informal practices by negotiating one comprehensive or several smaller service-provision agreements. Doing so would advance their collective objectives of improving service delivery for the community of Teslin (Village of Teslin and Teslin Tlingit Council 2009). Some of the issues under discussion may require negotiation with, and inclusion of, the Yukon government as a signatory. Besides formalizing existing practices, both communities are also interested in negotiating formal agreements to increase water delivery to TTC lands outside the municipal boundary from once to three times a week; streamlining road maintenance and confirm the Yukon government's involvement in extending and upgrading Sawmill Road; formalizing fire protection arrangements and confirm the Yukon government's provision of fire protection services outside municipal boundaries; formalizing VOT's jurisdiction over animal and insect control until TTC wishes to enact its own laws in the future; and creating a collaborative land-use planning process to facilitate joint decision-making and economic efficiencies (Across the River Consulting and Urban Systems 2013).

At first glance, these issues seem to involve fairly low levels of engagement and intensity between the governments. A closer examination of these issues, however, suggests something much deeper and entangled.

On the comprehensive servicing agreement, for instance, some of the discussions involve the VOT and the TTC working as allies to attract the support of the Yukon government to provide important services within and outside the community, including upgrades to Sawmill Road and fire protection (Across the River Consulting and Urban Systems 2013). Similarly, the possibility of creating a collaborative land-use planning process for joint decision-making may generate regularized communication and interactions, and the ceding of land-use planning authority by each community. Indeed, the TTC and the VOT have already begun working on a joint land-use planning process, having created a nine-member working group comprising three members from the VOT, three members from the TTC, and three members from the community at large (Wirth 2014). The municipal boundary expansion is also interesting because it would increase the linkages between the TTC and the VOT by bringing more TTC lands into the municipality's jurisdiction. In return for the VOT's provision of services to these newly incorporated lands, TTC members living on these lands would gain the right to vote in municipal elections. Ultimately, the expansion of municipal boundaries would likely result in increased integration and cooperation in the form of each community ceding some additional political autonomy in exchange for the production of new collective and public goods.

Overall, and based on the nature of the formal agreements, the informal arrangements, and the issues under discussion, we argue that the city's relationship with the Teslin Tlingit Council should be classified as residing in the upper left quadrant of table 4.2 (strong synergy / high intensity and engagement). More specifically, the nature of the five formal agreements themselves are crucial markers and determinants of the highly intense partnerships between these governments because they commit them to cede some autonomy in exchange for the production and management of selected public goods (e.g. a skateboard park; recreation programming; etc.). As well, a survey of Village of Teslin council minutes from 2006 to 2014 confirms that both communities regularly engage in discussions with each other on a variety of issues.[16] These patterns have not gone unnoticed by outsiders and interested observers; during our fieldwork, one knowledgeable territorial official independently identified these communities as having the

---

16 We attempted to collect council meeting minutes from the other three cases in this study, but they were either not publicly available or were incomplete.

Table 4.2. Village of Teslin / Teslin Tlingit Council Relationship-Type Matrix

	Intensity	
Engagement	High	Low
High	Strong synergy	In the loop
Low	Agreement-centred	Business as usual

most developed and positive intergovernmental relationship in the territory (Smith, 2014). What explains this pattern of intergovernmental relations?

Analysis

Our theoretical framework and empirical evidence gathered from the field reveal that a variety of factors have contributed to the emergence of a highly engaged and intensive intergovernmental relationship between the Village of Teslin (VOT) and the Teslin Tlingit Council (TTC). These factors straddle the range of variables outlined in our theoretical framework. In some cases, the factors had a mainly positive and collaborative effect. In other instances, the factors simultaneously constrained and encouraged collective action.

Institutions

At their core, institutions provide constraints and incentives for collective action. In the TTC and the VOT, the institutions that structured their relationship were the Teslin Tlingit land claims and self-government agreements. In essence, these documents created a new and powerful actor in the area, the Teslin Tlingit Council, which was armed with an extensive range of rights, powers, responsibilities, and resources to deliver public goods to and on behalf of Teslin Tlingit citizens. Yet, in many ways, TTC's increased revenues were balanced by the sheer scope of its new powers and responsibilities, which are much broader than what is typically found among Indian Act–type band councils. In other words, although Indigenous governments, on the whole, tend to gain significant financial resources through self-government agreements, they must also take on additional responsibilities, which in turn can negate the impact of these additional revenue streams.

Nonetheless, the Teslin Tlingit land claims and self-government agreements provide both governments with some incentives to cooperate. Broadly speaking, although the mandates and jurisdictions of the TTC and the VOT are fundamentally different from each other, they also overlap, and in those instances there are opportunities for cooperation. One example is recreational programming and services. Both the VOT and the TTC have a legal and political mandate to provide recreational facilities and programming for their citizens. However, rather than each government building its own ice rink or skateboard park, they chose to work together to provide these public goods collectively, sharing the costs and the responsibilities for managing them (Curran 2014; Wirth 2014).

From the VOT's perspective, there is another reason why the land claims and self-government agreements encourage cooperation. Put simply, the TTC is a new and powerful actor in the region with more funds, members, powers, and influence than the VOT; in the words of one VOT official, the VOT is more like a junior partner to the TTC. By cooperating with the TTC, VOT officials believe that they can more successfully apply for and receive additional resources from senior levels of government to benefit the Teslin region as a whole. According to Gord Curran (2014), "For us, from a village perspective, TTC is huge. We're a junior partner. And ... it's lucky we have a great working relationship. I mean it ... they're a huge powerful First Nation, and ... I'm glad we have a great working relationship. I think it helps us. And I think it helps TTC as well." Moreover, "there's all kinds of ... projects that have happened that I don't think we could have done, just as a municipality ... they got the skateboard park, the fourth sewer main. Things like that ... They [the TTC] ... have a lot of pull in the Yukon. And ... as a result we feel it as well, in a positive way" (ibid.). In this sense, the VOT faces a strong incentive to work collaboratively with the TTC on a variety of issues and levels.

Beyond these general considerations and effects, there are also formal provisions in the agreements that create incentives for cooperation. Section 24.7 of the land claims agreement, for instance, reads "A Yukon First Nation, Canada, the Yukon and Yukon municipalities, may develop common administrative or planning structures within a community, region or district of the Yukon" (Teslin Tlingit Council 1993b, s. 43). Similarly, section 26 states that the Teslin Tlingit Council can enter into agreements with municipalities "to provide for such matters as municipal or local government services joint planning, zoning or other land use control." Any such agreement must address the costs of delivering that service, provide a dispute-resolution mechanism, and ensure that the First Nation pays a similar rate for the services "as are paid by property owners in the same or similar communities" (44). Finally, section 12 of the self-government agreement (13) allows the TTC to "delegate any of its powers, including legislative powers," to municipalities and other local bodies recognized under Yukon law. Overall, the land claims and self-government agreements provide a legal and political basis for the TTC and the VOT to establish formal intergovernmental agreements and informal arrangements with each other, and interviewees have confirmed the importance of these documents for doing just that (Armour 2014; Curran 2014; Smith 2014; Wirth 2014).

The land claims and self-government agreements also contain provisions that potentially constrain the ability of the two governments to directly cooperate with each other and coordinate policymaking. According to its self-government agreement, the TTC can enter into taxation agreements only with the Yukon minister of finance. Furthermore, section 223 (1) of the Yukon Municipal Act prohibits Yukon municipalities from providing any sort of "privilege or exemption from any tax, rate, or rent" (Across the River Consulting and Urban Systems 2013).

The combined impact of these two provisions seems to create a powerful barrier for the two communities to coordinate their taxation rates and policies to maximize revenue generation and encourage specific types of economic development. That has certainly been the case. On the other hand, interviewees from both communities have indicated that taxation constraints have also encouraged cooperation between the communities. For instance, one observer commented,

> The way the village annual funding works is they get a huge grant from the government and then the rest is raised through property taxes, but the property taxes raise a minimal amount of money, as you can appreciate. I mean, there's not a lot of people that live here ... So that doesn't generate a lot of cash, so financially they [the VOT] can't necessarily afford to run all the infrastructure that we have. So they reach out to the other local government and say, ... "Here's our situation, you know, if we want to carry on with this, we need your help" ... the arrangement is to try and partner with them as much as possible, with each other. (Wirth 2014)

Rules affecting taxation, therefore, have not yet been an insurmountable barrier to intergovernmental cooperation.

Overall, the institutional climate has been favourable to intergovernmental cooperation. Indeed, it may not be coincidental that all intergovernmental agreements signed by the TTC and the VOT have occurred after the signing of the Teslin Tlingit comprehensive land claims and self-government agreements. These important documents seem to have created powerful incentives and opportunities for the communities to engage in collective action.

Resources

The availability of resources is another important factor in facilitating cooperation between the communities. In general, both communities are relatively small and have limited resources. Comparatively speaking, however, the TTC has more resources (e.g., its 2014–15 core operating budget estimate was $12,410,662; see Teslin Tlingit Council 2014a, 4) and citizens (approximately 800), compared to the VOT (budget numbers are not publicly accessible; population of approximately 150 + 300 TTC citizens), but it also has many more responsibilities and an enduring lack of capacity, at least in the sense that almost all new governments struggle at the beginning with establishing the necessary human, financial, and organizational resources to carry out their responsibilities. The VOT, on the other hand, benefits from having been a municipal government for many decades, which means it has had time to develop the necessary experience and capacity for providing a range of municipal services and programs. Both communities recognize these dynamics and comparative advantages and have tried to work together to produce public goods for the benefit of both communities (Curran 2014; Smith 2014; Wirth 2014).

The negotiations surrounding the proposal to expand the municipality's boundaries illustrate these dynamics. Recall that an external report in 2013 suggested that although the proposal would increase VOT but reduce TTC revenues, it would still produce a net increase for the communities as a whole. At that point, it would have been logical for the TTC to end discussions immediately. Instead, negotiations continue because the communities value the possibility of generating a collective net benefit for the entire Teslin community. Similarly, the two governments in 2011 collaborated on a recreation contribution agreement because it made sense from a resource perspective to work together, rather than producing parallel recreational services. According to one VOT official, the skateboard park, which serves residents from both communities, is an example of an initiative that simply could not have been built by the VOT on its own and without the financial support of the TTC (Curran 2014). The TTC was happy to work with the VOT on this issue, partly because its youth wanted the park built on village lands, but also because the VOT already had the infrastructure to manage it. A similar logic underpins how the two communities have managed animal control. Although the TTC has the authority to exercise this jurisdiction on its land, it has been happy to work instead with VOT by-laws and officials on this issue. The TTC has no reason to create its own animal control program when the VOT already has an effective program (Across the River Consulting and Urban Systems 2013).

Overall, both governments struggle with limited resources but also offer each other different sorts of comparative advantages in the production of collective and public goods (Curran 2014; Smith 2014; Wirth 2014). According to one First Nation official (Wirth 2014), "I think the village has a limited amount of money, right? ... this is a community of five hundred people, right? And for us to have the infrastructure that we have costs a significant amount of money. So in order to maintain this infrastructure, we need to have partners," and the most logical partner is the TTC, given that "a lot of the citizens that use these facilities are First Nation citizens." Similarly, a Yukon government official noted that "the First Nation's responsibilities are so much broader ... [and so they might not be able to provide] those specific services of recreation, water, sewer, landfill. The town does those things really well," so it makes sense for the TTC to work with the VOT to provide those services to its lands and citizens (Smith 2014).

External Intervention

Surprisingly, none of the Teslin interviewees were able to identify any federal or territorial interventions that might have encouraged or discouraged the TTC and the VOT from cooperating with each other. Our search of media reports and other publicly available documents confirmed this finding. Interviews with territorial officials, however, indicated that their government was interested in facilitating more cooperation and has hosted networking conferences, invited guest speakers, and delivered presentations on potential best practices, all of which were aimed mainly at First Nation governments. They have also, when asked, provided briefings to newly elected or appointed municipal officials about their neighbouring First Nations, but most of the time these officials seek out that information directly from their Indigenous counterparts. The territorial government has also recently launched several initiatives that may, one day, indirectly affect the TTC's and the VOT's intergovernmental relationship. One recent initiative involves the territorial government building an asset-management database for all municipal and Indigenous governments in the territory, but this project is still in its initial phases and none of the Teslin interviewees mentioned it (Armour 2014; Smith 2014; K. Taylor 2014). Overall, the data suggest that external interventions have had little effect on the evolution of the VOT's and the TTC's intergovernmental relationship.

History and Polarizing Events

A number of interviewees noted that the communities have always had a relatively strong and friendly intergovernmental relationship with each other, especially from 2005 onwards. According to an external report (Across the River Consulting and Urban Systems 2013, 2), "There is a strong history of collaboration in community planning (a joint Integrated Community Sustainability Plan was completed in 2009) and the delivery of services." Put simply, the five formal agreements since 2005 and the informal arrangements governing the delivery of services to TTC lands reflect a fairly positive historical relationship between the governments, and no major breakdowns have poisoned the relationship. The positive nature of this historical relationship is made clear by an executive manager: "If one of the governments can't fund it [the recreation agreement] a certain year, or can't fund all of it a certain year, you know, maybe the other government takes a holiday at the same time for that amount or the whole year. I mean, it's a mutual arrangement. Both governments recognize that it's better to partner and move forward as opposed to going on your own" (Wirth 2014).

The one polarizing event that deserves mention is the signing of the land claims and self-government agreements in the mid-1990s. As already discussed, these two agreements created a new and powerful actor in the region, which in turn suddenly changed the incentive structures facing both communities on collective action. Beyond this event, however, there have been no other sudden exogenous or endogenous events that have shifted the incentive structures for collective action.

Imperative

By now, it should be fairly clear that officials from both governments share strong imperatives to cooperate and engage in deeper forms of collective action (Curran 2014; Smith 2014; Wirth 2014). Actors from both sides recognize that there are opportunities for collaboration and that highly intensive and engaged collaboration is necessary to address a variety of shared goals. The signings of the MOU and the Teslin ICSP were formal announcements by the governments that they shared common concerns and goals and that they intended to work closely together to address these issues for the collective good of both communities. According to a recent TTC newsletter (Teslin Tlingit Council 2014a, 8), "In small communities like Teslin it makes sense for the two governments to work together. A more holistic and collaborative approach based on a common vision gives both governments greater strategic leverage in achieving common community development goals in a cost effective and timely manner. The challenges Teslin and similar small communities face are almost always interconnected. Working together increases the local capacity to get the work done by saving time and energy. Significant coordination balancing multiple, inter-related priorities is required to achieve positive outcomes and use limited resources more effectively." Subsequent actions have put these commitments and imperatives into practice, such as the successful negotiation of three joint-management agreements in 2005 and 2011 (sewer, skateboard park, and recreation contribution), the frequency of informal and formal discussions by the governments on a variety of issues, through ad hoc or regular meetings (Curran 2014; Wirth 2014), and the emergence of integrative initiatives such as the creation of a joint planning process (Teslin Tlingit Council 2014a) and the proposal to extend municipal boundaries to include more TTC settlement lands.

The municipal boundary proposal nicely illustrates the importance of shared imperatives to cooperate. According to one village councillor, "Right now one of the things we want to start is, there's a boundary that goes through a house. Just the way it worked out. So actually just over here, you know, part of the road is out of the boundary and part of the road is inside the boundary and then someone's kitchen [falls right on top of] the boundary ... So, the idea was to sort of fix that. It's the same process whether you try to fix that or whether you want to take in a huge amount of the municipality. So once you start that sketch and then you start looking at other things, you go, well maybe we should, you know, go with the Fox Point which is a little subdivision outside of here … You know, if we're going to do that, and we know that … TTC wants to build houses and we want to expand, you know we'd love to have the community grow a lot, so … you might as well just do it all, right now" (Curran 2014). Overall, both communities and governments see many advantages to working collaboratively, using deep forms of partnership to address their individual and shared goals, needs, and priorities (ibid.; Wirth 2014).

Community Capital

Although all factors identified so far have been important in creating both incentives and constraints for collective action, by far the most important factor has been community capital. Recall that community capital refers to a shared civic identity marked by social integration and the presence of community leaders who champion cooperation. In many ways, the Teslin region is a prime example of how strong community capital can generate intergovernmental cooperation marked by high levels of engagement and interaction.

Because of the territorial proximity of the communities, the frequency and nature of interactions between community members is both high and deep. Interviewees mention how community members use each other's facilities interchangeably. All community events, whether they are held on VOT or TTC lands, tend to be open to and attended by everyone (Wirth 2014). The annual Teslin Mini Rendezvous, for instance, involves members from both communities engaging in a variety of winter and Aboriginal-themed activities. Moreover, both Aboriginal and non-Aboriginal businesses and associations support and sponsor the event (Teslin Tlingit Council 2014a). As well, generally speaking, VOT and TTC borders are invisible to most community members. Recall that the building of a new skateboard park occurred on VOT lands, because that is where the TTC youth wanted it built. Similarly, Gord Curran (2014) notes,

> Someone had to tell me [where the VOT and TTC borders were], and I worked for TTC for three years … It's just not obvious to me. Now for those that have lived here a long time, they … could tell you, you know, the village … used to be very segregated. The village is over by the TTC health and social; … you go by the RCMP office, and towards the health centre and you turn in, just before the health centre. And then you're into

one of the older parts of town lots of [Department of Indian Affairs] housing. That's considered the village. And you know, in the past, historically,
there was definitely an imaginary or real line there. Since I moved to the
community, five, six years ago, I don't see the lines. So I think it'd be really
hard to tell if you're on settlement land or not on settlement land, and I
think there's a fairly high degree of integration … on the whole.

This social integration is also present among Teslin community leaders. Leaders from both communities frequently champion intergovernmental cooperation. According to Village Councillor Curran (2014),

There is a lot of communication. I mean, we all live in the same community …
I'll see the other councillors, informal that way. But I do know the CAO
and the executive director for the village and the executive director for the
TTC, they talk fairly frequently on different matters and then bring it up to
council's attention. So, you know, there's a lot of that informal stuff. Some
small stuff and big stuff, but there is sort of a constant stream of communication and working together. So it's hard for me to articulate this issue or
that issue … I think we've caught up to the TTC; their philosophy is we're
here for the community, period. And they do try to do their best to … be a
community organization now, they're there for their citizens, but they also …
know they're in Teslin, part of Teslin. The municipality's here and they do
try to, you know, make sure that … everyone's included.

Contributing to the strong community capital between the VOT and
the TTC leaders is the fact that these leaders frequently move back and
forth between the two governments. Current VOT Mayor Clara Jules,
for instance, has held her office since 2003. Before that, she was a VOT
city councillor and member of the Teslin Tlingit Council for fourteen
years (Gillmore 2012). Similarly, Wes Wirth was the CAO for the VOT
before he became executive manager for the TTC. Gord Curran, another
interviewee, worked for the TTC before becoming a VOT councillor.
Yukon government officials also mentioned how VOT mayors and
councillors are frequently TTC citizens and eventually work for both
governments at some point in their careers (Armour 2014; Smith 2014;
K. Taylor 2014). This frequent movement of officials between the two
governments not only contributes to a sense of shared civic identity, it
also generates a set of leaders who are interested in championing intergovernmental cooperation in the region. The result is an environment
conducive to the formation of partnerships.

Conclusion

In this chapter, we presented a case study from Yukon Territory in which two governments had forged an intergovernmental relationship marked by high levels of engagement and intensity. Our analysis of the data suggests that most of our framework's factors contributed to the emergence of this deep relationship. The land claims and self-government agreements radically changed the institutional structure governing the communities and the incentives facing their governments, creating new opportunities for cooperation. A radically more powerful TTC meant that the communities now shared a number of complementary comparative advantages. A general history of positive relationships and geographical proximity created powerful imperatives for deeper forms of collective action. Finally, the presence of significant community capital allowed the governments to first negotiate a relationship-building framework before embarking on highly intensive cooperative efforts, including formal agreements, informal arrangements, and ongoing discussions about a wide range of issues. Barring any sudden polarizing events, it is likely that this highly collaborative and intense intergovernmental relationship will endure and develop for many years.

Chapter Five

In the Loop: Village of Haines Junction and Champagne and Aishihik First Nations

In this chapter, we examine the intergovernmental relationship between the Champagne and Aishihik First Nations and the Village of Haines Junction, both of which are located in Yukon Territory. Our research shows that these two communities have developed a strong and friendly relationship with each other, characterized mainly by high levels of engagement. The intensity of that relationship, however, is much weaker than what we found in the previous chapter. The Village of Haines Junction and the Champagne and Aishikhik First Nations have concluded seven partnership agreements: four service agreements and three relationship-building MOUs. These agreements have not, however, generated any type of formal joint governance or joint-management structure or process. As such we characterize their relationship as an instance of the "in the loop" variety, marked by an engrained community practice of keeping the lines of communication open and frequent but without formal joint governance.

As in the previous cases, the framework factors had different impacts on the development of inter-community relationships, with the exception of community capital, which had a generally positive impact. In this case several factors constrained the capacity of the two communities to establish deeper partnerships – particularly those that required significant financial commitments. Treaty status (e.g., institutions) again played a role in creating a new and powerful actor (the Champagne and Aishikhik First Nations), but its power and authority applied to a much wider geographical area, thereby somewhat diminishing the importance of their relationship with the Village of Haines Junction (especially in comparison with the VOT/TTC case in the previous chapter). In addition, both staffing and financial limitations (e.g., resources)

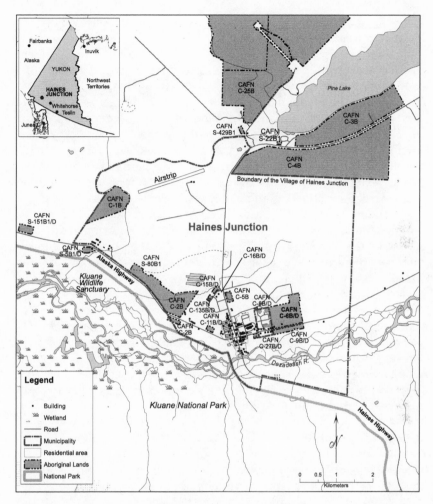

Figure 5.1. Village of Haines Junction and Champagne and Aishihik First Nations

constrained the capacity and the willingness of partners to engage in projects or agreements requiring joint management. While both communities could see opportunities for deeper and further collaboration, our investigation demonstrates that these tended to be in smaller projects for which incentives for engagement were poorly aligned (e.g., imperatives). As such, despite a generally positive community capital context, the political will to expand or deepen this relationship has been relatively weak.

It is again worth cautioning that, in the context of this study, the in-the-loop partnership type is not inherently better or worse than the two previous ones ("business as usual" and "strong synergy"). That this constellation of contextual factors has produced numerous functional agreements is significant, and we are interested primarily in the patterns that produced them rather than in judging their outcomes. Further-more, as with the other mixed-partnership type ("agreement-centred," discussed in the following chapter), this type of partnership may be less stable than the previous two over the long run. Strong communication between communities can ultimately lead to a deeper formalization of partnerships, and vice versa, particularly where community capital is strong. There is evidence that this may, in fact, be occurring in this case: the most recent relationship-building MOU is the broadest document and sets the groundwork for shared governance. However, since the details of how it will be implemented have yet to be worked out, this case remains an in-the-loop partnership. It is also worth noting that another outcome, unique to this variety, is also possible. In this type of partnership, informal collaboration and communication may effectively *substitute for*, rather than stimulate, formalized cooperation. Rather than creating joint institutions, the partners may instead opt to keep infor-mation flowing and to come together only when and as needed without a formalized framework of collective governance. This case may be an interesting instance of a community in transition.

Community Profiles

The Village of Haines Junction, Yukon Territory, is located approxi-mately 160 kilometres west of Whitehorse at the junction of the Haines and Alaska Highways and adjacent to the Kluane National Park and Reserve. The community has a population of approximately six hun-dred, of whom fewer than half are Champagne and Aishihik First Nations citizens. The village utilizes a typical municipal government structure. On the political side, a mayor and four councillors exercise executive and legislative functions, while a chief administrative officer (CAO) oversees a small bureaucracy (receptionist, treasurer, and sev-eral other "front-line" officials). Community facilities include a K–12 school, a Yukon College campus, a public library, a small airport, a rec-reation complex (which includes an indoor ice arena, swimming pool, playground, and basketball court), and a variety of government buildings (federal, territorial, and First Nations). The village also houses a variety of small businesses (inns and motels, restaurants, tourism outfits, general contractors, etc.) and tourist attractions (Haines Junction Visitor Reception Centre, St Elias Convention Centre, and the Village Monument).

Surrounding the Village of Haines Junction are the traditional territories of the Champagne and Aishihik First Nations (CAFN). At one time, these two First Nations were distinct groups, but sometime during the middle part of the twentieth century, the federal government amalgamated them into one Aboriginal community. Today, the CAFN maintains the plural form of "Nations" in their title to reflect their historical duality.

The community's membership is relatively large and spread out among several regions in the territory. According to the CAFN's draft Integrated Community Sustainability Plan (Champagne and Aishihik First Nations 2014, 5–7), the community has about 710 citizens; 202 live in and around the Village of Haines Junction (140 on settlement lands; 62 off settlement lands), 22 in the community of Canyon (which is about thirty kilometres from Haines Junction), 17 in Champagne (which is about sixty-five kilometres from Haines Junction), 80 in Takhini (which is about forty-five kilometres from Whitehorse), and 353 in Whitehorse. Much like the Teslin Tlingit, the CAFN are also a self-governing Indigenous group, having completed a comprehensive land claims agreement and a self-government agreement in 1995. These documents put into practice and modify many of the general provisions set out in the 1994 Umbrella Final Agreement (UFA), which was negotiated and ratified in March 1993 by the Council of Yukon Indians on behalf of all fourteen Yukon First Nations in the territory (Alcantara 2013, 86–7).

Much like the Teslin Tlingit, the CAFN were also part of the initial group of four Yukon First Nations to complete an individual final agreement in 1995. Under the terms of its land claims agreement (Champagne and Aishihik First Nations 1993a, chap. 9), the community received title and jurisdiction to over 1,230 square kilometres of Category A land (surface and subsurface title), 1,165 square kilometres of Category B land (surface title only), and 31 square kilometres of reserve land. These are the same amounts of lands that the Teslin Tlingit Council received in its settlement. The CAFN also received $27,523,936 to be paid over fifteen years, as well as a range of rights and responsibilities over economic development, fish and wildlife, special management areas (e.g., Kluane National Park, Sha'washe and the surrounding area), heritage, and other land-related issues (ibid.). Under its self-government agreement (ibid.), the CAFN also secured a comprehensive range of governance-related matters. Some of these jurisdictions include health care, education, social and welfare services, training programs, childcare, inheritance and wills, administration of justice, solemnization of marriage, use and management of settlement lands, transportation, and taxation. Much like other self-government agreements, the CAFN has the right to determine when and exactly how it will exercise authority over these areas.

To put these new powers and responsibilities into practice, the CAFN drafted and ratified a constitution. This foundational document lays out the structure, organization, and public administration of the CAFN's new government. It also contains rules governing the rights and responsibilities of citizens, elections, and the management of public revenues, expenditures, and assets, among other things (Champagne and Aishihik First Nations 2012). An important provision in the constitution states, "There shall be no sale of any settlement lands" (pt 3, s. 63). The CAFN government operates under an Aboriginal self-government model as opposed to the better-known public (government of Nunavut) model.

The formal structure of the CAFN government is organized around four different branches, each of which exercises some combination of executive, legislative, and/or administrative functions. The seven-member chief and council, which is made up of the chief, four councillors-at-large, one elders councillor, and one youth councillor, exercises executive and legislative powers. Chief and council members generally serve four-year terms, are elected directly by CAFN citizens, and are responsible for one or more portfolios. For instance, in 2013, Chief James Allen oversaw the secretariat and finance, while Councillor and Deputy Chief Dayle Macdonald was responsible for education, health, and social services. In some instances, two councillors can share authority over one portfolio, such as Councillors Mary Jane Jim and Harold Johnson, both of whom were responsible for lands and resources in 2013. Generally speaking, chief and council (also known as the First Nations Council) have the authority to "enact, amend, and enforce any and all legislation ... raise, invest, expend and borrow money," establish a judicial and legal system, and enter into treaties and agreements with other governments, organizations, persons, or corporations (Champagne and Aishihik First Nations 2012, pt 2, s. 52). This branch is perhaps the most important and influential one because of the range of powers at its disposal.

In terms of the other branches, the CAFN General Assembly, which meets annually, is made up of a quorum of at least forty CAFN citizens (although all citizens are invited to attend and participate), a quorum from chief and council, and selected delegates from six "ridings" representing citizens living in the CAFN communities of Takhini, Klukshu,[17] Champagne, Canyon, Haines Junction, and Whitehorse. Among other things, the general assembly holds the other branches accountable by providing them with direction (e.g., through resolutions), receiving updates on programs, activities, and services, reviewing financial activities, amending the constitution, and setting government mandates (Champagne and Aishihik First Nations 2012, pt 2, ss. 22–4). The Elders Senate is made up of all CAFN citizens aged sixty years and older. This branch provides advice to the other branches and has the power to appoint an interim member to chief and council to ensure that a quorum is met, should the chief or a councillor be unable to exercise appropriate duties for some reason (pt 2, ss. 57–8). Finally, the Youth Council also provides advice to the other branches and is made up of all CAFN citizens between the ages of sixteen and twenty-three (pt 2, ss. 60–1). In addition to these government branches, the CAFN government has departments to help the branches carry out their duties. These departments include community wellness, education, executive council, finance, governance, human resources, lands and resources, language, culture, heritage, and property services.

Current Agreements and Intergovernmental Issues

The Village of Haines Junction and the CAFN government have signed seven formal agreements with each other over the last two decades (see table 5.1). Four are jurisdictional-negotiation partnerships that address service provision and three are relationship-building agreements (e.g., memorandums of understanding). In general, these agreements reveal an intergovernmental relationship characterized by relatively high levels of engagement and low levels of intensity (see table 5.2).

---

17 This community is essentially a seasonal use area. Very few citizens live here permanently.

Table 5.1. Village of Haines Junction and Champagne and Aishihik First Nations Inter-governmental Agreements

Agreement	Date	Type	Substance
Animal control and services	1995–2001	Service agreement	VHJ to provide CAFN with animal control in exchange for a fee
Water and sewer	Early to mid-1990s	Service agreement	VHJ to provide CAFN with water and sewer in exchange for a fee
Fire protection	Early to mid-1990s	Service agreement	VHJ to provide CAFN with fire protection in exchange for a fee
Solid waste	Early to mid-1990s	Service agreement	VHJ to provide CAFN with solid-waste removal and storage in exchange for a fee
MOU on dialogue	Mid-2000s	Relationship building	VHJ and CAFN agree to meet quarterly to discuss issues of common concern
MOU on economic development	Late 2000s	Relationship building	VHJ and CAFN agree to meet regularly to coordinate economic development activities
MOU on dialogue	2014	Relationship building	VHJ and CAFN agree to meet annually to discuss issues of common concern

Table 5.2. Village of Haines Junction and Champagne and Aishihik First Nations Relationship Matrix

	Intensity	
Engagement	High	Low
High	Strong synergy	In the loop
Low	Agreement-centred	Business as usual

The four jurisdictional negotiation agreements, none of which are publicly available, are essentially service provision arrangements addressing things like animal control (see Village of Haines Junction and Champagne 2014, 3), water provision and sewer treatment, fire protection, and solid waste (Crawshay 2014; Gervais 2014; Riseborough 2014; Rufiange-Holway 2014; Wright 2014). All of these agreements were signed during the early to mid-1990s and have long since expired. Nonetheless, the VHJ has continued to provide these services to CAFN settlement lands in and around Haines Junction, and the CAFN government has continued to pay for them; indeed, interviewees from both sides have indicated that the CAFN has paid every bill submitted to them for these services over the last two decades (Crawshay 2014; Riseborough 2014; Rufiange-Holway 2014). In more recent years, there have been active discussions about renewing these agreements, and indeed updated versions are with the CAFN under legal review. Although VHJ officials had not yet received word on the status of this review, neither they nor the CAFN officials were concerned about the delay. Both sides are generally satisfied with the current informal arrangement and so are in no rush to formalize the new agreements[18] (Gervais 2014; Rufiange-Holway 2014).

The VHJ and CAFN have also signed three memorandums of understanding (MOU), of which only one (Village of Haines Junction and Champagne and Aishihik First Nations 2014) is publicly available. These documents aim to foster a stronger and more productive relationship between the two governments. The first MOU, signed in the mid-2000s, commits the parties (e.g., chief and council, and mayor and council) to meet regularly (approximately two to four times a year) to discuss issues of common concern (Riseborough 2012). The second MOU, signed in the late 2000s, commits the parties to discuss the possibility of crafting a regional economic development strategy centred on "the feasibility of using local biomass as a fuel source for local electrical energy and heat generation, and in conjunction with other partners, acquisition of a piece of federally owned property (about 80 acres) which was an experimental farm in the 1940s and 50s with a view to attracting an education facility or a 'clean and green' research and development centre to the site" (Riseborough 2012). The third MOU, signed during the summer of 2014, was to update and replace the previous MOUs (Crawshay 2014; Gervais 2014; Rufiange-Holway 2014; Village of Haines Junction and Champagne and Aishihik First Nations 2014). The preamble of this

---

18 If the parties were happy with the status quo, then why would they seek renewal of the formal agreements? Some interviewees answered that they had seen other previously positive relationships in BC "go south" for one reason or another. As a result, the interviewees believed that they should at least try to renew the agreements to mitigate some of the consequences should something similar happen in Haines Junction in the near future.

new agreement mentions the close proximity of the communities, their historical relationship with each other, and the fact that the CAFN government has a duty to serve all of its citizens, including those living in Haines Junction (Village of Haines Junction and Champagne and Aishihik First Nations 2014, 1). This MOU also commits the parties to:

- hold joint council meetings at least once per year (with the meeting location alternating between the two communities);
- negotiate a list of joint projects to be pursued;
- facilitate regular contact between government officials from both communities;
- try and work together on planning exercises;
- pursue joint interests as they relate to federal gas tax revenues;
- discuss the possibility of drafting a regional economic development plan; and
- assess all existing and future service provision agreements and arrangements between the two communities. (Village of Haines Junction and Champagne and Aishihik First Nations 2014, 2)

Overall, these formal agreements indicate a relationship marked by relatively high levels of engagement and low levels of intensity. The low intensity stems from the fact that the completed agreements are essentially service-provision arrangements. The high engagement is the result of the MOUs, which commit the politicians to meet regularly to discuss a wide range of issues. Although the required number of formal meetings has declined over the years (from quarterly gatherings in the mid-2000s to annual ones in 2014 and onwards), the promise to hold *yearly* joint council meetings is still substantially more than the number of formal joint council meetings that have been held or are scheduled to be held between the city of Sault Ste Marie and its neighbouring First Nations governments in Ontario (zero). Significantly, while the MOUs commit the leadership of both communities to regularized meetings, they have not (yet) established any formalized governance mechanisms (such as joint economic development plans). As a result, this relationship remains an in-the-loop type, despite the fact that the MOUs have consistently expressed the intention to establish a more intense governance relationship.

Our initial characterization of the VHJ's and the CAFN's intergovernmental relationship is confirmed by our analysis of their informal interactions and the issues they have discussed over the years.

Although the formal agreements indicate a decline in formal engagement at the joint council level, interviewees report that informal interactions between staff and political leaders from both sides have increased over the years. This is especially true in the last year or so, and there is much optimism that the number of informal interactions will continue to increase over the next several years (Crawshay 2014; Gervais 2014; Rufiange-Holway 2014). According to a former CAO of the VHJ, Michael Riseborough (2014), when he was CAO, he would communicate via email or phone with CAFN officials (mostly with Terry Rufiange-Holway, CAFN director of property services) approximately two or three times a month as issues arose. Most of the time, these matters involved the water system (e.g., a broken water pipe) or animal control (e.g., "dogs running wild"). He would also meet with CAFN officials to discuss and coordinate emergency preparedness (Riseborough 2014; Rufiange-Holway 2014). According to Mayor Crawshay (2014),

> We do a joint emergency measures planning exercise as well, which is another really important one. So that, because we have to recognize what each government can do. I mean if there's a forest fire threatening Haines Junction, all the municipality has to worry about is this community, because that's our mandate. Champagne Aishihik has to worry about the people at Canyon, the people at Takhini, anybody staying at Klukshu. They've got a much larger area that their service has to be diluted over, to protect their citizens. So that's an important aspect of something like an emergency measures joint planning exercise ... You need to understand that we can't take municipal equipment outside the village of Haines Junction as easily as Champagne Aishihik can take their municipal equipment down to Klukshu and save ... that community. So ... it's just understanding each other's limitations ... but it's so valuable.

(See also Government of Yukon 2011.) In the past, CAFN and VHJ staff members have also had numerous meetings to discuss potential economic development initiatives, including the purchase of an old experimental farm and the creation of a biomass energy and heat-generating facility. None of these discussions, however, have produced an agreement.

The high frequency of informal meetings has continued under the new CAO, Keir Gervais. Since his hiring in early 2014 and at the time of our interview in July 2014, he had already met informally with CAFN staff several times to discuss issues as they had arisen. For example, Gervais (2014) had

> reached out to Amy [McKinnon, CAFN communications manager] and said, I learned that Champagne Aishihik used to be part of an advertising opportunity that's available to us. It's a magazine called the *Mile Post* ... and it's a vacation planner for people who travel along the Alaska Highway. It's a bible. It's just the most magnificent publication you can ever get your hands on. And I learned that Champagne Aishihik used to be in it. It came before me ten days ago. I was rather disappointed in how the village of Haines, how much money the village of Haines Junction had spent and what we had received and I had my own ideas for a redesign ... And when I learned that Champagne Aishihik used to [partner on the advertisement], but hadn't recently, I reached out to Amy to say, this is my vision for a two-page spread and I'd really like Champagne Aishihik to be part of it. She liked it.

CAFN and VHJ staff members have also met recently to discuss other areas of cooperation. Shortly after being hired as CAO, Mayor Crawshay arranged an informal lunch meeting with his new CAO, CAFN Chief James Allen, and CAFN Director of Property Services Terry Rufiange-Holway, to discuss possible joint ventures. At that meeting the decision was made to sign a new MOU to replace the previous ones (Crawshay 2014; Gervais 2014; Rufiange-Holway 2014; Village of Haines Junction 2014). Several weeks later, Rufiange-Holway approached Gervais about partnering on a housing development. The village owned residential plots in the south end that had yet to be developed, so the CAFN was interested in developing the lots for private and social housing. The officials agreed to discuss the proposals with their leaders. In short, officials from both sides are optimistic that although the number of formal joint-council meetings has declined over the years, frequent informal meetings continue to occur and in fact may increase over time.

Overall, our analysis of the formal and informal agreements and interactions between VHJ and CAFN indicate a relationship that is marked by high levels of engagement but low levels of intensity. Officials from both governments are interested in cooperation and see the relationship as mainly positive, even though the substance of the interactions has yet to develop into an intensive partnership. According to VHJ CAO Keir Gervais (2014), the relationship between the two governments "appears to be fine, ... paraphrasing Chief Allen's comment

to me a couple of weeks ago, 'We haven't been to court yet' (*laughing*) ...
it is a good sign ... And I think how you and I just laughed about it,
is how he intended it to be. It's a good sign." Similarly, CAFN Policy
Analyst Skeeter Wright (2014) observes, "Everything I've picked up
about Haines Junction and Champagne Aishihik is that they work very
well together." Yet, for the most part, interactions between officials have
been mainly informational rather than substantive. Again, according to
Gervais (2014), "I would summarize it [the relationship] right now from
my information I've gathered, is that ... we're strong on planning and
we've been weak on follow through." In the next section of this chapter, we provide some reasons for why this particular intergovernmental
pattern exists in the Haines Junction region.

Analysis

A variety of factors have contributed to the emergence of a highly
engaged yet weakly intensive intergovernmental relationship between
the Village of Haines Junction (VHJ) and the Champagne and Aishihik
First Nations (CAFN). Many of the same factors affecting the communities in Teslin are also present in the relationship between VHJ and
CAFN, producing both enabling and constraining effects on collective
action. In the section below, we concentrate mainly on the important
unique factors that have produced a highly engaged yet weakly intensive intergovernmental relationship. An overarching theme is the (negative) effect that having multiple CAFN communities with significant
residents has had on CAFN decision-making, resource allocation, and
imperatives for collective action.

Institutions

Much like in Teslin, the relevant core institutions that have exerted a significant influence on the relationship between the VHJ and the CAFN
are the CAFN land claims and self-government agreements. These documents created a new and powerful actor in the region, especially when
compared against the typical Indian Act band council. With these agreements, the CAFN are now armed with an extensive battery of rights,
powers, responsibilities, and resources to deliver a broad range of public goods. Much like in the Teslin Tlingit Council case, the emergence of
the CAFN as a self-governing nation with a treaty-protected land base
created both opportunities and constraints for collective action.

Yet there are several important institutional differences between the Teslin Tlingit Council and the CAFN cases. One major difference is that the CAFN have community subdivisions beyond those in and around Haines Junction. As Rufiange-Holway (2014) notes, "We have four main communities, which is this one here [Haines Junction], you go out thirty kilometres and that's our Canyon Creek. From Haines Junction you go fifty miles and that's Champagne, which is halfway between Whitehorse and Haines Junction. And ... so you go from here a hundred kilometres it's our Takhini River subdivision, which is fifty kilometres from Whitehorse ... So again, everything that we have as far as projects, programs, planning opportunities, it's spread out over those communities" (see also Crawshay 2014; Wright 2014). The existence of these multiple residential areas means that political representation and decision-making must account for these other communities and their individual interests, which may be quite different from CAFN's interests in and around Haines Junction. In the Teslin area, by comparison, "We [Teslin Tlingit Council] do not have other inhabited communities like CAFN – the closest similarity would be Fox Point subdivision but it is only four kilometres away. The municipality actually provides some services to that area on a fee-for-service basis, even though it is [just] outside the boundary. We would provide the rest of the services that are not provided by VOT" (Wirth 2014).

Another important difference between the Teslin Tlingit Council (TTC) and the CAFN is the status of their settlement lands within municipal boundaries. According to its comprehensive land claims agreement, TTC settlement lands within municipal boundaries are also municipal lands, which means that the Village of Teslin provides them with municipal services. As well, TTC citizens and residents on these lands are allowed to vote in municipal elections, among other things. In contrast, CAFN's modern treaty states explicitly that CAFN settlement lands within the municipality (called Block 30) are completely separate from municipal jurisdiction. Interviewees describe CAFN lands within Haines Junction as a series of "doughnut holes," and as a result, the CAFN has chosen to develop a number of municipal style services, such as a road maintenance department, to service these areas, which in turn somewhat limits the possibility for cooperation (Rufiange-Holway 2014; Wright 2014). According to Mayor Crawshay (2014),

The positive effect from a First Nation perspective is that they were able to develop, I mean out of necessity, their own municipal public works department to manage the streets and roads and garbage pickup ... right now that department is maybe three or four people, so those are First Nation citizens working. So it was an employment opportunity that was specific to First Nation citizens. So that was a real advantage ... it's Champagne and Aishihik First Nations government generating work for its citizens. So that was a positive step ... the downside is that there's a certain amount of redundancy in equipment and in infrastructure. Like if we were plowing streets for the whole place it would probably be cheaper for us to do the whole town, including Block 30, than to have Champagne Aishihik do their own and us do our own, because ... that same equipment has to go out to Canyon, Champagne, Takhini, and ... their municipal responsibilities, or their equivalent of municipal responsibilities is stretched over other communities, where it's sort of easier for us.

According to CAFN officials, the development of parallel services was not only the result of their modern treaty, (and specifically the provisions that created the "doughnut holes"). Also important were CAFN concerns about the potential negative financial impact that might occur if it partnered with the municipality to deliver these services. According to Riseborough (2014),

The bottom line is that we don't have a store. Now in the community we have elderly people, and the First Nation has elders who don't drive or who are sufficiently incapacitated through age that they may not be able to drive. So a fellow from the First Nation came over to me and said, "Look, we're thinking about buying a bus so that we can bus the elders in to Whitehorse. Would the village be interested in, you know, coming in a partnership on this?" ... We've got a number of people ... that are in their eighties that need to do their shopping and whatnot. We thought, what a good idea. But with changes to the financial transfer agreement, that occurred a number of years back, all of a sudden I got a phone call from Terry and he said, "You know what, if we go into partnership with you, you being the village, then what that does, is, it puts us offside of the financial transfer agreement and we'd have to pay tax on a bunch of stuff." There are hidden things in the agreement that may not really be on the surface, that once we get into it, prevent us from doing things together.

However, these fears appear to have been misplaced and perhaps had more to do with a lack of familiarity with the text of the modern treaty. Indeed, as mentioned in the previous chapter, there are provisions in the land claims agreements that allow Yukon First Nations to get around these barriers. According to Rufiange-Holway (2014),

> RUFIANGE-HOLWAY: Section 26 [of the modern treaty] relates to local service agreements. Yeah, so we, this department just used that this past winter for the very first time. It has been around for twenty years and this is the first time we ever used it … the concern always is that if Champagne and Aishihik provides services off their settlement lands, … we may go offside with our taxation status. So we could lose millions of dollars for a thousand-dollar job.
>
> INTERVIEWER: Right, so if you provide some sort of service for Haines Junction, off settlement lands, you could lose revenues because of the financial transfer agreement?
>
> RUFIANGE-HOLWAY: Exactly. So with that [s. 26] now we can look at utilizing … the tool to allow us to work cooperatively with local governments for service provisions … that's what section 26 says, that you have to provide municipal services at a cost-recovery basis. Yeah. That's a tool I'm going to use further.
>
> INTERVIEWER: OK. So why hadn't you used it previously to that? Was there just no need or you just weren't aware of it?
>
> RUFIANGE-HOLWAY: Well, it was one of those dusty things on the shelf (*laughing*). Similar to before, we didn't have a problem with … doing a contract for Champagne and Aishihik … Because of our new requirement for FTA, when we do our FTA renewal there's financial capacity reporting (FCR) requirements. So there's where … the FCR came in and highlighted the taxation requirements and reporting requirements, that's where it all of a sudden became a big deal … So we had the CACC [Canadian Association of Crown Counsel], the CACC lawyer, our lawyer, and YG guys looking at it going, OK, what's going on here? Then of course you've got everyone going, I can't believe it's taken this much and it's this hard to do. There's got to be another way. So all of a sudden, that's when the section 26 popped up. And that deal was very easy to do.

Overall, the self-government and comprehensive land claims agreements have had a positive and negative effect on cooperation. Although these agreements contain provisions similar to those in the Teslin Tlingit agreements, several important differences (e.g., the greater number of CAFN communities to service/represent and the existence of Block 30 settlement lands) have limited the opportunities for substantive cooperation between the two governments. In that sense, the institutional environment generated by the modern treaty (in conjunction with other factors) has created a context that is conducive to conversation and dialogue, but less so for substantive and intensive cooperation.

Resources

Much like in the Teslin region, the Village of Haines Junction government is quite small (especially compared to the CAFN government), and while the CAFN is certainly larger than the village government in its financial and human resources, these advantages are counterbalanced by the broad range of responsibilities it has gained under its agreements and the many communities it must service. According to a CAFN annual report (2007, 11), "Municipal infrastructure is very costly to provide and maintain, and even more so because we supply services to four communities spread out over a wide area." Similarly, Mayor Crawshay (2014) notes, "The Village of Haines Junction has got six employees in public works, three in the office. You know, it's a fairly small organization. Champagne/Aishihik has far more employees but they're covering their whole traditional territory. I mean, they're completely maxed out as far as capacity for what they have to do. If somebody takes time off, their door is closed for as long as they're away. And if that person happens to be the director of lands and resources, nothing happens." The demands on CAFN political leaders are especially significant. CAFN councillors representing citizens in Canyon, Champagne, and Takhini spend most of their time in those communities, working and advocating on behalf of their constituents, so opportunities for collaboration in Haines Junction must compete with the priorities and problems facing these other communities (Wright 2014). CAFN Chief Allen faces even larger constraints on his time, as he must balance CAFN regional interests (e.g., the different CAFN subdivisions) with his responsibilities in Whitehorse, representing the CAFN in territorial and national forums (ibid.; Riseborough 2014).

One complication is the limited resources available to the Village of Haines Junction (VHJ). Much like the Village of Teslin, the VHJ is blessed with infrastructure built up over the years, but lacks significant financial resources. For instance, there were discussions with the CAFN and other stakeholders about purchasing an old experimental farm and turning it into a satellite campus of Yukon College or a research-and-development centre (Crawshay 2014; Riseborough 2014). At first, the municipality was interested in partnering on the purchase but quickly pulled out in response to the cost. Similarly, the VHJ and the CAFN governments spoke about the possibility of investing in a biomass facility for producing electricity and heat. However, the VHJ quickly backed out once it became clear that its financial contribution would have to be in the range of $400,000, a sum that was far too large given the VHJ's limited resources (Crawshay 2014; Riseborough 2014). As a result, the CAFN is pursuing a scaled-down version of the biomass facility on its own to provide heat and energy for its cultural centre.

In short, the resources available for collective action in this region are fairly limited. Specifically, in addition to the resource complications generated by the financial-capacity reporting requirements discussed in the previous section, small local budgets and the existence of multiple CAFN communities significantly reduce the potential scope for collective action. Hence, all completed formal agreements with the CAFN have been service provision arrangements. Co-management and co-funded partnerships have yet to emerge, partly because of these various resource constraints.

External Intervention

Similar to Teslin, none of the interviewees could identify any senior level interventions that had a significant impact on their incentives or capacity to cooperate. Interviewees did mention that both communities received federal gas tax revenues through the territorial government and that they had fulfilled the legal requirements to access those funds. As well, there were some very preliminary and exploratory discussions about coordinating their use of these funds for a number of joint ventures, such as the proposed biomass facility. However, none of those discussions have generated meaningful or substantive collective action (Rufiange-Holway 2014). For the CAFN, again a major constraint on collective action is the existence of multiple CAFN communities. According to Terry Rufiange-Holway (2014), "There's a desire to look at projects that are going to benefit the community through shared contributions of gas tax funding. Of course, the limitation for Champagne and Aishihik is that it's not our only community." For the VHJ, the gas tax money was a valuable resource to be spent on municipal projects. According to Michael Riseborough (2014), "The guy that was on the biomass thing, ... the pointman ... was an ex-executive member of the Northwestel team ... a fairly sharp guy, but he made some assumptions that we would be prepared to use, like $5 million of our gas tax money to put into that, and that wasn't going to happen. I basically told him that from the outset … The mayor and council simply had other plans for that money." In short, external interventions have had a negligible impact on the intergovernmental relationship in Haines Junction, as the result of resource constraints and political representation demands.

History and Polarizing Events

Similar to factors relating to external interventions, there was little evidence or mention of any factors relating to history or polarizing events that had an impact on the relationship between CAFN and VHJ. Generally speaking, interviewees from both sides indicated that the historical intergovernmental relationship between the two communities has been positive but also uneventful (Rufiange-Holway 2014; Wright 2014). Former CAO Michael Riseborough (2014) spoke about a history and culture of trust between the two governments. A prime example of this positive history of working together is the previously mentioned provision of municipal-style services to CAFN lands, all of which has been going on for some time without formal agreements. According to Riseborough (2014), "My preference as a bureaucrat would be to have something on the file that's got everybody's signature on it. The fact that it's not there reflects a different way of doing business … [and it] hasn't been a concern to us because they've been honouring their side of what we've been doing. You know, whatever we've provided for, or whatever, they've paid for. So it has not become an issue at this point … [and] I don't anticipate that it will become an issue in the future."

Imperative

Generally speaking, the relationship between the two governments is fairly positive. Staff and politicians from both sides suggest that there is a good working relationship between the governments; indeed, the interviewees generally characterize this relationship by referencing the relatively frequent interactions they have with each other, mostly informal, but also at formal levels. Despite this generally positive relationship, a key factor that seems to be missing from this case compared to the Teslin one is a strong imperative for deeper forms of collective action. Although officials from both sides have mentioned a variety of possible joint ventures, either as abstract ideas that they would like to pursue, or more tangible issues that they have raised with their partners, there does not seem to be any strong motivation from either side to pursue a more substantive relationship or partnership. There seems to be a divergence in what each government sees as its main priorities, and as a result, each side's proposal for joint action tends to be a low priority for the other party.

A good example of this dynamic is the VHJ's landfill site, which the current CAO of Haines Junction identified as one of his top priorities to address this year. The landfill has recently seen a significant increase in the amount of hazardous waste being dumped there, somewhere "to the tune of a couple of hundred thousand dollars" (Gervais 2014). Although the increase in hazardous waste has nothing to do with the CAFN, he hopes that perhaps his government can negotiate some sort of joint partnership with them to better manage the landfill. This partnership might take the form of the CAFN and the VHJ working together to hire and fund new employees to manage the site. Another priority mentioned by VHJ officials was emergency preparedness (Gervais 2014), which might take the form of clarifying who is responsible and who should pay for what in the event of a major emergency. For the CAFN, however, their interviewees did not mention either of these issues as potential or important avenues for cooperation. Instead, they talked about the importance of housing for the community (Champagne and Aishihik First Nations 2007; Habitat for Humanity Yukon 2012) and the need to approach the Village about building private and public housing on VHJ lands (Rufiange-Holway 2014), an issue that none of the VHJ interviewees mentioned.

Imperative was also missing at a recent meeting between senior officials from both sides. Although interviewees from both governments spoke highly of the meeting, going so far as to say that significant progress was made at fostering dialogue and strengthening the relationship between their governments, nothing of substance beyond the 2014 MOU was produced, nor has any sort of joint priority list or joint venture agreement been negotiated or signed. Still, this lack of substantive outcomes does not mean that the relationship between both governments is unhealthy or negative. Yet a strong but perhaps unrecognized obstacle is a substantial divergence in the goals that each government has prioritized for joint action. As a result, the parties share a weak imperative for deeper forms of partnership.

Community Capital

Much like in the previous chapters, community capital is an important factor in determining the character of the intergovernmental interactions between the Village of Haines Junction and the CAFN government. Comparatively speaking, the amount of community capital in this region is relatively more than and less than what exists in the Sault Ste Marie and Teslin regions, respectively. This finding mirrors in many ways the different levels of intergovernmental engagement and intensity found in each of these three regions.

Recall that community capital refers to a shared civic identity marked by social integration and the presence of leaders in both communities who champion cooperation. In Teslin, social integration was high and facilitated by the close proximity of the two communities. Interviewees discussed the reality of an "invisible border" and the frequent interaction and participation by members from both communities in community events and programming. In contrast, Sault Ste Marie and its relationship with Batchewana and Garden River First Nations seemed to suffer from high levels of racism, despite daily interactions between Aboriginal and non-Aboriginal citizens.

In Haines Junction, social integration is clearly much higher than in the Sault Ste Marie region, but somewhat less than in Teslin. The main reason for this difference, especially with respect to Teslin, is probably due to the fact that a relatively large number of CAFN members live in other communities outside of Haines Junction. For instance, despite working for the CAFN government in Haines Junction for several years, one interviewee was not familiar with the community dynamics and facilities in Haines Junction because the interviewee lived elsewhere. Nonetheless, Aboriginal and non-Aboriginal residents of Haines Junction still seem to interact positively and frequently at a variety of events and venues in and around Haines Junction. According to Gervais (2014),

> Then you look at our proximity to each other, I mean, we're right here, right? Like, we're right here in bed together … I really mean this, I have not seen any evidence whatsoever of any unharmonious inter-community relations. To put that into context, sometimes … I've been in other communities where there's sort of a visible or verbal lack of respect for the … other culture … I have not seen that [here] … for example, I was here for Canada Day. You know there's an excellent, excellent mix of people at Canada Day … sometimes those are the type of indicators you can see where you've got an event

like that and you look across the audience and you don't see a single Aboriginal person and you go, "Oh, OK, interesting. OK so we've got this community but we really don't have this community." I didn't see any of that ...
I swim every morning in the pool. I see users in the pool ... I'm making an
assumption that I'm seeing Champagne Aishihik residents using the pool,
people using the pool. So yeah.

Other interviewees agree with these sentiments. During our interview, Mayor Crawshay (2014) discussed numerous instances of positive social interaction in Haines Junction. For instance, "Right now we
spend $200,000 a year on recreation. And we don't say, 'You're First
Nation, you can't come in.' It's for the whole community. Well, Champagne Aishihik recognized that well OK, there's no sense in us dupli-
cating an arena or a swimming pool or a curling rink. So they put in a
youth centre and a day care that's available for the whole community ...
The youth centre is for the whole community ... So there's a pool table,
there's music, there's magazines, there's games. And it's well used by
the whole community." Michael Riseborough (2014) concurs with these
sentiments and suggests that this strong sense of community can facilitate collective action between VHJ and CAFN leaders: "When there are
opportunities that are mutually beneficial, there's certainly an intention
to work together. An important thing ... is that ..., we all live together
here. And you see people on the street, so you stop and talk to them.
You know, it doesn't matter if they're Champagne Aishihik citizens or
not. Everybody's sort of friendly with each other." Moreover, "I'm not
sure that we really differentiate between CAFN and the municipality. I
mean, everybody lives here, and if there's an advantage to doing something or talking about something, in particular when it comes to recreation, and particularly if it's something that's been spearheaded by the
volunteers, it just happens."

In addition to a strong sense of community integration, and much
like in Teslin, community leaders frequently act as champions for cooperation. Former CAO Michael Riseborough (2014) mentioned that he
frequently encountered Chief Allen in the community and would talk
to him about work and non-work issues in a variety of places and situations in Haines Junction. Mayor Crawshay (2014) mentioned that he
owned a business in Haines Junction, called Kluane Machine, which
services vehicles and heavy equipment, and that CAFN Chief Allen
was a frequent customer, so they would speak regularly about a variety of work and non-work related issues. Similarly, CAFN Director of

Property Services Terry Rufiange-Holway (2014) noted a similar relationship with the mayor: "I can just phone him and say, 'Hi Mike, how are you?' You know, I talked to him as Mike of Kluane Machine. 'Oh, Mike, is there a mayor there? (*laughing*) Oh, can I talk to the mayor now, right?' That kind of thing." These types of connections and interest in cooperation, while present in the region in previous years, are much more apparent now, especially with the current VHJ and CAFN leadership.

Finally, another important difference between Haines Junction and the previous cases is the frequency in which leaders move back and forth between the governments. In Sault Ste Marie, interviewees indicated there was little to no movement. In contrast, the governments in Teslin seemed to have their officials move much more frequently between governments. In Haines Junction, however, interviewees report little to no movement. The only example that the interviewees could think of was VHJ City Councillor Angie Charlebois, who worked for CAFN Chief Allen many years ago. None of the interviewees could think of any other politicians or staff who had worked for both governments.

Overall, community capital in this region seems stronger than in Sault Ste Marie but weaker than in Teslin. Although the Village of Haines Junction and the Champagne and Aishihik First Nations seem to share a relatively strong civic identity, it is also weakened by the fact that the CAFN has other communities outside of the region that it must serve. Moreover, although these communities do have leaders who champion intergovernmental cooperation, the evidence suggests they have fewer champions compared to Teslin. These differences may partially explain why the VHJ and the CAFN have an in-the-loop relationship.

Conclusion

In this chapter, we presented another case study from Yukon Territory. In this instance, the two governments had forged an in-the-loop intergovernmental relationship marked by high levels of engagement but low levels of intensity. Although a number of factors contributed to the emergence of this relationship, our analysis of the evidence suggests that institutional, resource, imperative, and community capital factors were crucial. More specifically, although both communities have faced strong incentives to engage in fairly regular dialogue and to seek cooperation, factors relating to resource constraints, different representational responsibilities, and the weak imperative for joint action have acted as powerful constraints on collective action beyond basic municipal service-style partnerships. It is possible that more intensive partnerships will emerge if new and more influential external interventions or polarizing events push the governments to prioritize similar goals. If this happens, we may see the emergence of stronger imperatives for joint action and subsequently the emergence of more intensive partnerships. Until then, it is likely that the status quo will continue into the near future.

Chapter Six

Agreement-Centred: Regional Municipality of Les Basques and Malécite de Viger First Nation

Low-engagement but high-intensity partnerships, where partners have deep institutional ties but interact infrequently, are relatively rare in our database, partly because there are fewer high-intensity partnerships overall and partially because partnerships of any kind, formal or informal, seldom emerge without prior interaction between partners. They are also likely rare because of their inherent instability. A partnership negotiated in this context can either fall apart quickly or naturally lead to more intense engagement – as such, it is possible that this agreement-centred, low-engagement, high-intensity state was simply an ephemeral and transitory phase for some of the partnerships documented in our database.

The case of the partnership between the Québécois Regional Municipality of Les Basques and the Malécite de Viger First Nation for the joint management of the Inter-Nations Regional Park, concluded in 2014, enables us to study one such moment. This partnership commits the members to create a jointly controlled and financed non-profit organization to manage the development and promotion of the park. However, this relationship emerged without any prior formal, and negligible informal, contact between the leadership of the two governments.

This case stands out from the others in this study in several other important respects. First, while the other case studies involved cooperation between Indigenous and municipal authorities, this partnership was negotiated with a second-tier municipality: a regional county municipality. This scale of authority is common across Quebec (and indeed has analogues in other provinces) and is responsible for, among other things, regional planning and environmental management. As such, the creation and administration of regional parks falls under the legal purview of this scale. The Malécite de Viger First Nation is also unique: it is one of the few First Nations in Canada that has claim to reserve territory but whose citizens live exclusively off-reserve. The Malécite population lacks significant residential concentrations characteristic of other First Nations, which has entailed several unique governance challenges. A final distinguishing characteristic of this case is the presence of a villain in the form of a private hunting and fishing club – the Club Appalaches – that has legally and physically opposed the agendas of both communities to increase access to public lands that make up the park network. As such, institutional asymmetry (institutions) has, until recently, limited interaction between community governments, but this barrier was overcome by a combination of a powerful common enemy (a clear, pressing, and common imperative) and strong community capital. The absence of serious resource constraints also contributed to the capacity of both parties to engage in the partnership.

This case is significant in that it suggests that where there are few links between Indigenous and neighbouring authorities, a strong imperative for cooperation can provide an important catalyst for productive and intensive relationships where other conditions, such as community capital, are amenable. This case also supports the contention that this type of partnership is inherently unstable and may function more as a transition stage than a permanent condition.

Community Profiles

The Regional Municipality of Les Basques (hereafter referred to simply as Les Basques) is a regional municipality located in the Bas-Saint-Laurent region of eastern Quebec (see figure 6.1). It covers an area of 1,115 square kilometres and contains a population of 9,184 (Ministère d'affaires municipales et Occupation du Territoire Québec 2010). Les Basques is one of eighty-seven regional municipalities in the province and functions as a regional tier of administration in charge of regional planning and management, support for local economic development, and coordinating emergency planning, among other responsibilities (Ministère d'affaires municipales et Occupation du Territoire Québec 2014). The region contains eleven local governments (municipalities, villages, and parishes) and is administered from the largest: Trois-Pistoles.

The Basques region's location near the mouth of the St Lawrence River has intimately shaped its history and economy. The region's name is derived from that of Basque Island near the southern shore of the

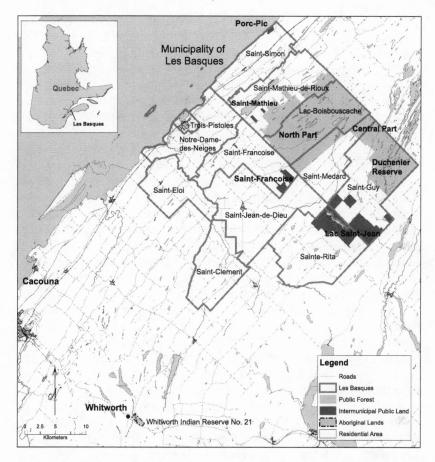

Figure 6.1. Regional Municipality of Les Basques and Malécite de Viger First Nation

river, so named by the seventeenth-century Basque mariners who plied the waters in pursuit of whales and seal. Despite the name, most modern inhabitants do not claim Basque ancestry (Chez les Basques 2014). The Lower St Lawrence region in which Les Basques is situated is predominantly rural – over 63 per cent of the population lives in rural areas (Ministère d'immigration diversité et inclusion Québec 2014) – and its economy is closely tied to natural resources and extraction. Key industries include forestry, fishing, manufacturing and resource processing, marine and biotechnology, and eco-tourism. The Les Basques capital, Trois Pistoles, contains just over a third of the region's inhabitants and is best known for the Notre-Dame-des-Neiges church, built in 1885.

The Malécite de Viger First Nation (MVFN) are an Algonquian-speaking Indigenous community of the Wabanaki Confederacy with a traditional territory that extends across the north and south shores of the St Lawrence River and up to the Bay of Fundy in the provinces of Quebec and New Brunswick. The Malécite have historically been a nomadic people scattered relatively thinly across their ancestral territory and, as such, were not formally recognized as a First Nation by the Canadian or Quebec provincial governments until 1987 (Calderhead 2011). Before their formal recognition the Malécite people endured several centuries of disappointment and displacement. In the early nineteenth century, the Department of Native Affairs granted the Malécite around seventy acres of territory in the Isle-Verte region, which they cultivated when hunting and fishing migration cycles permitted. However, as population pressures mounted in the region, the government reclaimed what they viewed as underutilized land in 1869 for new colonization. From this point the landless Malécite people were dispersed and much of their traditions were lost to history until a small group of 130 Malécite united in 1987 to petition for formal recognition as a Québécois First Nation. As part of this process the Malécite were accorded two small reserves at Cacouna (near the municipality of Cacouna) and Whitworth (about thirty kilometres south of Rivière-de-Loup); none of the 1,121 citizens reside in these territories (Aboriginal Affairs and Northern Development Canada 2014). Both reserves are located within the boundaries of the Rivière-de-Loup Regional Municipality, directly contiguous to Les Basques. A sizable population of Malécite, however, inhabits Les Basques territory in and around Trois-Pistoles. The Cacouna Reserve, at 0.4 hectares, is the smallest reserve in Canada. This Indigenous diaspora, as Calderhead and Klein (2012) describe it, is governed by a band council that maintains its own records of Malécite citizens.

Despite the challenges of a dispersed population, the band council is very active in the development and preservation of the Malécite culture, economy, and community. Since its inception it has established several companies to enhance Malécite autonomy and support economic development. The Toku management company was established in 2011 as a non-profit company whose mission is "to put forward economic development measures that will generate revenues and wealth which, in turn, will create sustainable growth that will produce new opportunities, new choices for the community, a greater autonomy and a means to reach self-sufficiency" (Première Nation Malécite de Viger 2013a). The Commercial Fisheries Enterprise Management Committee was formed in 2009 to coordinate commercial and food fisheries operations, personnel recruitment and training, to provide financial assistance, and to plan fisheries expansion. The committee aims to support the Malécite populations involved in fisheries as well as the communities of the Lower Saint Lawrence region (ibid.).

The band council and broader Malécite community are also engaged in an ongoing project of territorial expansion in an effort to establish a territorial centre in which to concentrate the community and community activities. The tiny Cacouna Reserve is the administrative seat of the council but is not large enough to be permanently inhabited by a significant Malécite population. The band continues to negotiate with the federal government for additional land to be added to the Cacouna Reserve, although numerous barriers to expansion (such as the limited amount of available land) hinder the process (Calderhead and Klein 2012). Documents dated 2014 indicate that there are also comprehensive land claims processes underway but that they are still in very early stages of development (Dallaire 2014).

The centrally administered but widely dispersed Malécite de Viger First Nation has enabled the community to become an active and visible presence in Les Basques economic and cultural development and to forge important relationships with municipal and other governmental partners. Our research indicates that the relationship between the MVFN and Les Basques regional municipality are intensifying as a result of the development of the regional park project.

Existing Agreements and Intergovernmental Issues

The MVFN has several informal agreements and connections with municipalities in the Les Basques region. These include the "Two Nations, One Celebration" annual festival that celebrates the history of the village and reserve of Cacouna – two separate and neighbouring territorial entities that share a name. The celebration aims to foster the history and heritage of both communities and attempts to create an activity to "bring people together, to develop a feeling of belonging and to promote the discovery of the two cultures" (Première Nation Malécite de Viger 2013c). The MVFN is also a partner in several tourism and development projects. The municipality of Rivière-de-Loup has included the MVFN in the Carrefour Maritime port lands planning and development initiative. This project envisions the sustainable development of the Rivière-de-Loup port area and of tourist facilities to accommodate cruise ship passengers, aquatic clubs, a museum, and a marine park (Calderhead and Klein 2012).

However, to date it only has one formal agreement with the Les Basques regional municipality government: the agreement for the creation and management of the Inter-Nations Regional Park (see figure 6.1). The agreement, signed on 19 August 2014, commits the partners to work together to create a non-profit organization to consolidate the management of public park areas accounting for over 256 square kilometres of land within the region and maintain them for public ecological, hunting, fishing, and other recreational uses (Conseil de la Première Nation Malécite de Viger et La Municipalité Régionale de Comté des Basques 2014). The object of the partnership is to effectively unite all of the lands available for public use in the region to augment access, collectively manage the natural resources, and improve infrastructure maintenance (e.g., trails, shelters, and tourist attractions).

This agreement is one of the most intense formal partnerships included in this book. Not only does it commit the partners to collaborate on the ongoing management of the designated public territories, it also requires them to set up a formal body to do so and to share funding obligations to support the park directorate. Project funding is split equally between the partners. Each party agreed to contribute $20,000 to the initial start-up costs in the first year, primarily to support human resource needs and a project coordinator. Les Basques has also pledged $50,000 per year for 2015–17, while the MVFN has committed to provide the same sum for 2015 and 2016.[19]

This level of administrative and financial collaboration entails a relatively large sacrifice of autonomy for both parties and indicates a strong formal partnership. What is unique is that this partnership emerged without much prior history or current examples of interaction between the leadership of the two governments. As such it is classified as an agreement-centred relationship (see table 6.1).

---

19 An election in 2016 prevents the MVFN from committing substantial funds beyond that year.

Table 6.1. Regional Municipality of Les Basques / Malécite de Viger First Nation Relationship Matrix

	Intensity	
Engagement	High	Low
High	Strong synergy	In the loop
Low	Agreement-centred	Business as usual

Analysis

This low-engagement but high-intensity partnership emerged from the confluence of several unique circumstances. On an institutional level there are fewer opportunities for an administratively localized Indigenous government to interact with a regional scale of government. The cost of the partnership itself was also relatively cheap, and the funding to sustain it has not been difficult to access for either party. There has also been, perhaps most importantly, a very strong imperative for cooperation rooted in the perception that presenting a powerful and united front on access to public lands would result in a more effective offence against a common enemy: the Club de chasse et pêche Appalaches (hereafter referred to as the Club Appalaches). This institutional context, resource profile, and imperative, combined with relatively strong community capital in the form of strong leadership and inter-community relations, enabled the creation of a strong partnership in a context of weak overall engagement.

Institutions

On an institutional level there have been very few opportunities for Les Basques and MVFN leadership to develop a formal or informal relationship. As a regional – second tier – level of government, the regional municipality is responsible for few issues of relevance to the MVFN. Most service-provision and infrastructure-maintenance competencies are couched at the local scale. Most MVFN interactions are therefore aimed at individual municipalities, if and when the administration interacts with local authorities at all. Furthermore, the dispersal of MVFN citizens and the extent of MVFN traditional territory beyond the borders of the small regional municipality means that, like in the Villages of Haines

Junction/CAFN case discussed in the previous chapter, the MVFN administration has traditionally focused on a much larger geographical area within which Les Basques is just one of many actors. Where interactions were reported, they were characterized as in passing – co-attendance at large meetings of regional elected officials (such as the Conférence Régional des Élus) or at provincial consultations. Partly as a result of these different spheres of focus, it is not surprising that few opportunities for interaction have arisen until this point.

Resources

Resources are often cited as a barrier to the evolution of more intense partnerships between First Nations and local authorities. If not an outright impediment, the lack of or uncertainty about sourcing financial support has been at least a point of hesitation for actors considering deeper cooperation. The Inter-Nations Park project stands out as a rare exception to this overall trend. The willingness of the two governments to pool resources and share costs is particularly interesting, because the financial commitments, while not large, are certainly significant and extend over several years. This arrangement is a relatively strong indicator of the underlying commitment to the formal partnership over the long term.

Access to, and willingness to pool, resources has been aided in this case by several factors. First, both parties were confident that they would be able to source funding for the project from a combination of own-source and provincial grants. Second, in the case of Les Basques, a private member's bill from the Quebec National Assembly affirmed their legal right to spend public funds in support of a non-profit regional park initiative, thereby eliminating potential opposition from constituent municipalities. Finally, the substance of the agreement was such that the costs of the project are to be borne equally by both parties – an arrangement that all actors agree is equitable.

The MVFN has access to provincial funding from a variety of sources to support its participation in the project. In addition to standard revenue streams, MVFN officials have cited potential access to funding through a First Nations forestry-management participation program (Program de participation autochtone à l'aménagement forestier – PPA) administered by the provincial Ministry of Natural Resources. As a second-tier level of municipal government, the Les Basques regional municipality pools contributions from each of its constituent municipalities to finance regional planning and development projects. Interviewees reported that regional municipality income from these sources was sufficient to cover the costs of the project for the committed time period. None of the individuals interviewed in the course of this project expressed any concern that costs for the immediate project – the establishment and support of the non-profit park structure – would be a difficulty, now or in the future. Some did mention that funding was not immediately available for ancillary projects – an archaeological survey and a Malécite cultural interpretation centre.

Even when resources are available, that cooperation can often be derailed by disagreements about funding priorities. The Inter-Nations Park initiative enjoyed a relatively high degree of support from stakeholders associated with both local authorities and the MVFN and this meant that pooling resources was not a major point of contention. The main sources of opposition on financial grounds came from a few municipalities within Les Basques – principally from the current leadership of St-Mathieu-de-Rioux. Interestingly, these objections were not aimed at the validity of the Les Basques financial commitment to the park project but to the financial (and other) implications associated with one of the initiative's agendas to reclaim hunting and fishing rights to the territory for public use (this is discussed further in the imperatives section). The authority of Les Basques to spend its public funds on a collaborative project was also strengthened by a private member's bill (*Journal des débats* ... 2013) explicitly authorizing the regional municipality to create and fund a non-profit organization in partnership with actors that are not political constituents of its territory. This affirmation largely removed any legal objections that constituent municipalities may have had to the right of the regional municipality to spend collected revenues for the project.

In cases where the costs of partnership are low, disagreements can arise over the division of responsibilities. In this case the parties agreed very early on to a 50:50 division of costs, which has been warmly received by project proponents and stakeholders on both sides. It should be noted that while a 50:50 division appears as though it should be the most equitable solution in any circumstance, there is nothing inevitable about this conclusion. After all, this division of costs might not seem as fair for an actor who perceived that his partner(s) will reap more than half the benefit. As such, it is remarkable to observe such a high degree of consensus from all parties involved. All interviewees reported that they viewed this allocation of costs as "very fair."

In sum, resources have not been a significant barrier and have arguably been a substantial enabler of cooperation between Les Basques and the MVFN in the creation of the Inter-Nations Regional Park enterprise. While the partnership to create the non-profit organization and reorganize park territories under its aegis will certainly proceed, one financial matter remains unresolved: who will be responsible for the costs associated with recuperating the public right to hunt and fish on park lands from the Club Appalaches? To the extent that both parties agree that this should be a provincial responsibility, this outstanding financial question should not pose a significant barrier to sustained cooperation. However, should the bid to involve the province in resolving this dispute fail, resources may yet play a role in the evolution of this partnership.

External Intervention

Although external actors were consulted by both Les Basques and the MVFN while the partnership was being negotiated, none played a significant or direct role in cementing the project. According to interviews, the MVFN consulted extensively with the Secretariat of Aboriginal Affairs (SAA), the minister of Aboriginal affairs (MAA), and the Ministry of Natural Resources (MERN). Les Basques also consulted the Ministry of Aboriginal Affairs, the Ministry of Culture (MC), and the Ministry of Municipal Affairs (MAMOT). Most of these consultations revolved around two key issues: (1) the implications and duty to consult on the private member's bill enabling the regional municipality to create the non-profit organization to manage the park, and (2) the ongoing attempt to wrest control of hunting and fishing rights from the Club Appalaches as part of the Inter-Nations Park agenda. These provincial actors reportedly supported the initiative and clarified legal issues surrounding park competencies and ambitions. The most significant intervention by an external actor came in the form of Bill 206, the legislation that enabled Les Basques to create the non-profit park-management entity, but aside from this procedural action, no other external actors influenced the evolution of the partnership.

History and Polarizing Events

As previously mentioned, there have been few formal or informal interactions between the Les Basques administration and the MVFN community and, as such, the historical evolution of their relationship formally began with the negotiation of the Inter-Nations project. Rather than furnish context for inter-community relationships, history has provided a nearly blank slate. As a result, the parties had neither positive nor negative expectations of the reception they would receive heading into discussions surrounding the park. As one observer described it, "I had the impression that there had never really been formal relationships between the two communities ... there was really a lack of awareness on both sides" (Sanquer 2014). Other interview subjects stated more succinctly that there was simply "no history" between the parties.

That said, despite the lack of historical relations between authorities, both communities did share a struggle against the Club Appalaches – a conflict with deep and complex historical roots. The heart of the conflict is the unusual circumstance that hunting and fishing rights to some public land that makes up the Inter-Nations Park (and accounting for approximately 60 per cent of public lands in Les Basques territory) belong to a private club – the Club Appalaches. While the club cannot legally prohibit citizens from hiking or camping on the land, they can restrict access for hunting and fishing. However, there have been reports for decades that the club discouraged the public from accessing the northern part of the forest, and there were several incidents in 2010 and 2011 during which the private warden of the club intimidated individuals and groups as they pursued legal uses of the land resulting in formal legal complaints against the club (Première Nation Malécite de Viger et MRC les Basques 2013b; Radio-Canada 2013).

This unusual and contentious division of property rights on otherwise public land was the result of a preferential land deal between the owner, Lieutenant-Colonel Raymond Garneau, and the D'Auteuil Lumber Company in 1951, in which Garneau inserted a clause reserving "for himself and his heirs" hunting and fishing rights to the land in perpetuity (Huot 1999). The land, originally part of the seigneurie Nicolas-Riou (1751), had transferred to Garneau after several generations of pulp and paper corporations had used it for their industrial operations. D'Auteuil was the last and shortest-lived corporate owner. The land was expropriated by the Quebec government in 1953 and became part of the public domain in that same year, but the hunting and fishing rights, retained by Garneau and his heirs, did not transfer as part of the deal. Garneau ultimately sold his rights to the Club Appalaches in 1956 – a transaction that was ratified by a notarial act of the minister of lands and forests in 1956. The club itself had been active in the region since 1910, renting hunting and fishing access where it was available, until acquiring exclusive rights from Garneau.

Despite numerous attempts by local municipalities, provincial authorities, and later, the regional municipality to re-appropriate hunting and fishing rights, this bizarre division of rights has remained stubbornly intact. The most recent challenge, heard in the provincial court of appeal, was rejected in August 1999.

It is against this historical backdrop that Les Basques and the MVFN ultimately came to partner on the Inter-Nations Park. While no single polarizing event catalysed cooperation, the fact that both the regional municipality and the MVFN have consistently struggled against the challenges of public access imposed by the club has been extremely formative to the development of the partnership. The park initiative is a first step in a coordinated challenge to the dominance of the Club Appalaches.

Imperative

The common opposition to private hunting and fishing on public lands owing to the Club Appalaches unique property rights, and even more viscerally to the club's (sometimes violent) attempts to restrict public access to parts of this territory, has been a strong imperative to cooperation. Both communities abhor the negative treatment of their citizens and value the right of public access, but each also has its own agenda.

For the regional municipality, the goal of the park is, first and foremost, to assemble the total of public lands under one management structure and to ensure unmolested and complete access for all. For the MVFN, public access to Inter-Nations parklands is also bound up with historical land rights – these public lands were once part of their extensive migratory territory, of which they retain autonomy over only a tiny fraction of reserve-designated lands. Private control over the hunting and fishing rights on these otherwise public lands prevents the MVFN and its citizens from pursuing and exercising their own historical claims. For the MVFN, participation in the park initiative ensures that they have a voice in the land management and a partner in reclaiming traditional hunting and fishing rights.

Despite this alignment of interests, it is worth noting that cooperation was not the default position of the regional municipality when it embarked on the park project. In fact, the initiative originated from the Les Basques leadership, who pursued the private member's bill in the

Quebec National Assembly without consulting the MVFN. In public hearings on Bill 206, Amélie Larouche, counsellor for natural resources management for the MVFN, stated that MVFN leadership had heard of the initiative and the proposed bill only through the media and indicated that they had been "exasperated" to not have been consulted and cited a letter dated 5 March 2013 asking that the bill be rejected until proper consultations could take place (*Journal des débats* 2012). Ultimately, Les Basques recognized the benefit of including the MVFN in the park initiative because of their power with the provincial government and as an ally against the club. For their part, the MVFN recognized the benefit to overlooking the initial failure of Les Basques to consult, given that the park might serve as a vehicle to regain access to traditional hunting and fishing territories. Joint consultations did eventually take place in which the overall agreement for the park was settled, enabling the legislative process to proceed with the full support of both parties. Interestingly, only one of those interviewed mentioned this more convoluted path to cooperation, most preferring instead a more sanitized and harmonious narrative in which "in the process of consultations" about Bill 206 the actors logically came together to work as one.

For the MVFN, cooperation in the park initiative meant that they had gained a small victory: if the park was successful in reclaiming hunting and fishing rights from the Club Appalaches, as Les Basques hoped, the rights would not revert exclusively to the regional municipality (as had originally been the intention), but to a *joint authority* in which the MVFN has an equal stake. For its part, the regional municipality saw additional potential benefits to collaboration, beyond the advantages of cost sharing. Les Basques recognized that the MVFN had strong historical claims to hunting and fishing rights on the lands in question – much stronger than those of the regional municipality. Furthermore, as a First Nation the MVFN had the potential to influence the provincial government through different channels and with potentially more weight than the small regional municipality of Les Basques (Denis 2014). As such, both parties perceived that combining forces and working together strengthened their common goal – to ultimately defeat the Club Appalaches and regain public hunting and fishing rights – relative to working alone. As one stakeholder put it, "The regional municipality is much stronger politically now, as is the MVFN" (confidential interview 2014).

It is difficult to say whether the park would have gone ahead had Les Basques refused to consult or cooperate with the MVFN. One interviewee characterized the situation as potentially a no-win situation for Les Basques – Larouche and the MVFN had vowed to oppose any initiative that ran counter to their interests and traditional rights claims, such as Bill 206. Whether this opposition would have been enough to derail the enabling legislation is unclear. What is certain is that failure to consult would have marked a polarizing event in the MVFN–Les Basques relationship and constituted a black mark that would likely have shaped future interactions between the communities. Fortunately, the clear advantages of and imperatives for a collaborative approach enabled the development of a productive partnership. Whether this partnership will achieve the ends that both parties hope for in reclaiming property rights remains to be seen.

Community Capital

Considering the extensive dispersal of the MVFN community and lack of previous formal interactions between the leadership of both parties, community capital is significant, though not overly strong, in this case. What was most notable to the First Nations stakeholders in the process was the distinct lack of preconceptions and prejudices when dealing with the regional municipality and its agents. According to Larouche (2014), "There are often prejudices [from outsiders] dealing with First Nations, but we didn't see that with the Les Basques regional municipality." For the regional municipality it was striking that their First Nations partners were willing to deal with them as equals rather than treating them as a subordinate level of government: "First Nations are a higher level of government than us, they're closer to the provincial government. But we never got the impression that the band council thought that it was superior in these negotiations. We had a great relationship with the people that we worked with, and they never held their nationhood over us" (Denis 2014). Representatives of the regional municipality reported that they also worked very deliberately to make the MVFN delegates feel comfortable and respected throughout the process, even asking them to speak up if they ever felt taken for granted.

A relatively high degree of integration and low degree of visible separation between communities adds to the perception of collective stewardship of shared territories. Since all MVFN citizens live off the reservation, they are more naturally integrated into the communities in which they have chosen to settle. Some observers noted that one public official in the regional municipality had familial connections through marriage to the MVFN, but most dismissed this is merely a notable community overlap and did not characterize it as a significant political bridge. Connections between elected officials and community leaders were notably weaker in this case than in others in this study, though not entirely absent. The inclusiveness of MVFN economic development initiatives to non-Native residents – particularly in the realms of culture and fisheries – has also gone a long way to integrate the MVFN into, rather than separate it from, surrounding communities.

These factors, in addition to the neutral historical background discussed above, enabled leadership on both sides to approach negotiations with an open mind and a relatively high willingness to pursue cooperative solutions.

Conclusion

The Inter-Nations Park partnership is one of the most intense partnerships profiled in this study. The fact that it emerged from, and continues to exist, in a context characterized by low engagement outside of the formal arrangement is unique. This relationship configuration was possible because of the combination of low institutional opportunities for prior formal (or informal) interaction between communities; the ease with which parties were able to find, and willing to pool, the resources to support the joint organization that emerged; the strong imperative for cooperation furnished by the actions of the Club Appalaches; and relatively strong community capital owing partly to the natural dispersion of the MVFN community and its explicitly inclusive development policies.

Although several factors influenced development of this partnership out of a vacuum, this case effectively demonstrates the power of a strong imperative for cooperation. Without the catalysing (and antagonizing) presence of the Club Appalaches centred on hunting and fishing rights – a crucial piece in the MVFN struggle for autonomy by reclaiming traditional rights – the regional municipality may have been able to quietly create a park network on its own. However, because the stakes were so high, cooperation not only emerged, but emerged in its most intensive form – that of a jointly managed and financed organization. This most intensive form was the only one that could be acceptable to the MVFN seeking, as they were, legitimate claim to any rights transferred from the club to public authorities. While this is only a single case, it does suggest that where engagement has been historically low (or non-existent), intense cooperation can emerge if the imperative for cooperation is strong enough. A neutral historical background, close community integration, and ready access to resources add considerable weight to the endeavour.

As noted in the introduction, the high-intensity/low-engagement type of relationship is likely to be unstable – and there are already indications that this may be the case here. This instability stems from the fact that successful partnerships, such as the one formed around the Inter-Nations Park initiative, tend to stimulate partners to look for other opportunities for collaboration. One stakeholder described the negotiations as having "a snowball effect," while another asserted that links established between the two communities could facilitate exchanges in the future. Almost all stakeholders interviewed stated that they could envision more informal interactions and discussions as a direct result of the park partnership. As one noted, "We're getting to know each other" (Larouche 2014). As a result, this initial partnership may usher in a period of more intense engagement between these two communities and the initial low-engagement and high-intensity context may be only a transition period. Only time will tell.

Conclusion

We began this book by highlighting how many academics and journalists in Canada have tended to focus on the federal, provincial, and territorial levels when they write about the Indigenous–Crown relationship. In contrast, very little has been written on the quiet evolution that seems to be occurring at the municipal level between Indigenous governments and local authorities. To address this lacuna, our book attempts to describe and classify the Indigenous–local intergovernmental partnerships in Canada before identifying the salient factors that encourage them to emerge. To describe and classify these relationships, we constructed a matrix of four distinctive types based on two characteristics: engagement and intensity. Business-as-usual partnerships involve the parties engaging in infrequent communication and mainly service and business transactions. Strong-synergy relationships, in contrast, involve highly institutionalized partnerships and frequent communication. Agreement-centred partnerships are characterized by highly intense interactions but low levels of engagement. Finally, in-the-loop relationships involve low intensity but high levels of engagement.

In an ideal world, we would have used this matrix to analyse all Indigenous–local intergovernmental relationships in Canada. Unfortunately, such a task was too costly and difficult, given the realities of empirical research. Engagement and intensity can be discovered only by speaking with policymakers from each community, and this task was unfeasible, given the number of Indigenous governments and local authorities identified in our database as having some sort of formal agreement with a neighbouring government. Nonetheless, our framework and empirical findings do provide a useful starting point for studying these relationships and the different ways that Indigenous

Table C1. Summary of Factors

Type	Sault Ste Marie	Village of Teslin	Village of Haines Junction	Les Basques Regional Municipality
	Business as usual	*Strong synergy*	*In the loop*	*Agreement-centred*
Institutions	−	+	+/−	−
Resources	−	+	−	+
External intervention	−	+/−	+/−	+
History and polarizing events	−	+/−	+/−	+
Imperative	+	+	+/−	+
Community capital	+/−	+	+	+

− = negative effect on cooperation
+ = positive effect on cooperation
+/− = no effect or effects cancel out

governments and local authorities have been pursuing partnerships with each other.

Another goal of this project was to develop a theoretical framework that captured the range of possible factors that might encourage Indigenous governments and local authorities to engage in cooperation and partnership. Our framework, which we constructed deductively (Nelles and Alcantara 2014), contained six factors arranged along a continuum between capacity (the ability to engage in collective action) and willingness (the degree to which actors are disposed to invoke their capacities to act). Our case study research found that all factors had some effect on at least one type of Indigenous–local cooperation (see table C1); however, when we look at the influence of factors across the four types, it seemed that the factors related to willingness were more important than those related to capacity, regardless of the level of engagement and intensity of the partnership. In all four case study chapters, Indigenous and local government leaders shared at least some imperatives, resulting in formal/informal agreements for particular services (e.g., Sault Ste Marie, Teslin, and Haines Junction), communication commitments (e.g., Teslin and Haines Junction), and/or highly intense partnerships (e.g., Teslin and Les Basques). These results suggest that what matters for producing cooperation are the specific imperatives that communities have and the extent to which they align with each other (e.g., do they share an interest in housing for the region or does one community prioritize housing over roads and vice versa for the other community?).

Similarly, community capital was important in all four cases. The presence of a shared civic identity was crucial for encouraging the emergence of all four types of partnerships. Integrated communities and personal links between leaders in most of our case studies fostered a culture of openness to dialogue and collaborative proposals from neighbouring governments. On the other hand, the lack of positive links between leaders and the presence of general feelings of racism and hostility towards Indigenous peoples in Sault Ste Marie, despite frequent interactions between residents of both communities, meant stocks of community capital were generally low in the region. As a result, Indigenous and local leaders in this region were less predisposed to cooperate frequently and/or in intensive ways. Recall how some Indigenous interviewees felt that perceptions of racism and the existence of negative personal relationships between leaders affected how city officials treated their proposals and contract bids.

In contrast to imperatives and community capital, the other factors in our framework seemed to have mixed effects across the cases, and in some instances they had virtually no effect at all (e.g., external interventions, history, and polarizing events were generally absent in the Yukon chapters). In the case of the Village of Haines Junction and the Champagne and Aishihik First Nations, capacity had either a negative effect (e.g., resources) or a mixed effect (e.g., institutions and external intervention), while history and polarizing events were only slightly positive in fostering cooperation (e.g., generally positive but vague and uneventful). Instead, key factors were community capital, which was generally positive, and mismatched imperatives. Both communities saw value in cooperation, and dialogue and communication in particular, but the lack of strong community capital and aligned imperatives generated a relationship characterized by high levels of engagement but low levels of intensity.

Similarly, in northern Ontario, we found two sets of relationships that were characterized by low levels of engagement and intensity. In both cases, factors relating to capacity all seemed to have a negative effect on the emergence of a more intensive and/or more highly engaged partnership, as did most factors relating to willingness. The one exception was imperative. Municipal interviewees indicated that the city government viewed its neighbouring First Nations as being in no way different from other neighbouring local authorities who needed municipal services. As Sault Ste Marie Chief Administrative Officer Joe Fratesi (2013) remarked, "We have service agreements with them [Garden River and Batchewana], and we have service agreements with other neighbouring jurisdictions who are not First Nation, and we don't have regular meetings with them. If we have a service that we can provide, and they are prepared to pay for those services, and we can conveniently extend them, then we offer it to them ... [but] unless there is a need, we don't have communication with the township of Prince [or the First Nations]" (see also Apostle 2013). Similarly, First Nation interviewees from both communities did not mention any significant interest or strong need to partner with the municipality, beyond the bus route extension into Garden River First Nation. As a result, it seems that willingness, and especially the presence of complementary imperatives, is crucial for cooperation to emerge.

This finding is surprising but also novel and important, because it runs somewhat contrary to longstanding arguments in the literature on Aboriginal self-government and intergovernmental relations and policymaking. Much of the scholarship has tended to emphasize the importance of capacity and how many Aboriginal communities and governments lack sufficient capacity to deliver a wide range of programs and services to their band members and citizens (White, Maxim, and Beavon 2003; White 2009). Similarly, and of more relevance to this project, scholars writing about comprehensive land claims negotiations have noted that Aboriginal participants tend to be at a distinct disadvantage at the negotiating table because they lack the resources and capacity that the federal, provincial, and territorial governments have at their disposal (Alcantara 2013; Nadasdy 2003; Tully 2001). Finally, some reports by practitioners and non-governmental organizations on Indigenous–local relationships highlight the lack of capacity as a crucial impediment to the creation of partnerships (Federation of Canadian Municipalities 2011, 8, 10; Tamera Services Ltd. 2002, 22–2). Our case study findings, however, show that communities can still develop mutually beneficial relationships despite capacity and resource constraints. Indeed, willingness is a powerful incentive for the communities to find ways to overcome and/or maximize capacity weaknesses and differences to produce different types of Indigenous–local intergovernmental cooperation.

In this book, we have treated capacity mainly in a conventional way to refer to the human, legal, and financial resources that governments have at their disposal to engage in cooperative decision-making and implementation. Others, such as Howitt et al. (2013), argue that capacity should also be thought of in terms of the ability of non-Aboriginal actors to successfully navigate and integrate Indigenous knowledge and governance practices into intercultural processes and structures. For our case studies, however, this type of "Indigenous capacity" did not seem to have a significant role in generating the four types of relationships specified in our matrix. Instead, the presence of willingness factors such as imperatives and community capital were more important. Nonetheless, it may be that variables relating to Indigenous capacity can affect the presence and nature of the willingness factors identified in our framework. Future research will need to investigate the role of Indigenous-related capacity à la Howitt et al. (2013) for generating different types of Indigenous–municipal intergovernmental agreements and relationships.

Throughout this book, we have tried to remain neutral on the normative value (e.g., that cooperation, or different forms of cooperation, are what all communities should or should not always aspire to achieve) of the different forms of Indigenous–local partnerships that we found. Some readers may not be happy with this decision, but we think it is a defensible one, given recent trends in the scholarship on Aboriginal politics and public policy. As non-Aboriginal scholars, it is not our place to tell Indigenous communities how they should value or not value different forms of cooperation. Instead, our role is simply to provide a framework for scholars and practitioners to think more effectively about cooperation and the types of factors that go into encouraging different types of partnerships. As well, we do not think that cooperation between municipalities and Indigenous communities is appropriate on every policy issue. Instead, cooperation should be regarded as a strategic tool, depending on each community's preferences and capabilities. We consciously did not promote strong-synergy relationships, for instance, as being preferable to business-as-usual partnerships, because we recognize that a business-as-usual partnership may actually be preferable for some communities. Alternatively, in some situations there may be no real or strong need for collective action at all.

Others may want to build a normative argument for (or against) Indigenous–local intergovernmental cooperation on the basis of social justice, economic efficiency, or policy effectiveness, and we hope that they will use our book to take on this task. Our goals for this book, however, were quite different and reflect an established norm in political science that research can be strictly normative, explanatory, descriptive, or all three. We chose to write a book that provided a descriptive and explanatory analysis of Indigenous–local intergovernmental partnerships in Canada. In particular, we constructed a broadly applicable and generalizable framework for classifying different types of such partnerships and identifying the factors that contribute to their emergence. We leave it to others to take our work and situate it within the normative debates (Alfred 1999; Coulthard 2014; Flanagan 2008; Poelzer and Coates 2015; Widdowson and Howard 2008).

Nonetheless, our findings will still be of use and of interest to academics and policymakers. Provincial governments (e.g., Ontario Ministry of Municipal Affairs and Housing) and national organizations (e.g., Federation of Canadian Municipalities), among others (e.g., National Aboriginal Land Managers Association) have expressed a strong interest in finding new ways to encourage Indigenous–local intergovernmental partnerships in Canada. For senior levels of government, our findings suggest that they might consider creating opportunities that build capacity and foster willingness to encourage cooperation. For instance, they might create funding opportunities that privilege joint proposals from Indigenous governments and neighbouring local authorities. Doing so would provide these actors with additional capacity in the form of new financial resources and strong incentives to pursue collective action. These are the lessons from the Quebec and Yukon cases. Or they might create mechanisms to clarify the legal and moral responsibilities of Indigenous and municipal actors when they must deal with each other to address a variety of issues and interests (Andersen and Strachan 2011; Fraser and Viswanathan 2013; Murray 2011; Walker 2008). There is a real opportunity here, in particular, for Prime Minister Justin Trudeau and his government to put into practice their vision of a better relationship between Indigenous and non-Indigenous communities in Canada by providing a range of incentives and resources to Indigenous communities to forge more cooperative links with neighbouring municipalities.

For Indigenous and local political leaders, cooperation might be encouraged in several ways. Policymakers might redesign their decision-making processes so that they are compatible with their neighbours. Recall that municipal interviewees from the Sault Ste Marie cases indicated that different decision-making timelines and levels of autonomy at the civil servant level seemed to act as disincentives for collaboration. Streamlining these aspects, assuming that the actors see them as roadblocks to cooperation, should improve the likelihood of creating formal or informal partnerships between the communities.

Policymakers might also identify each community's comparative advantages and use them in their proposals for collaboration. In the case of the Village of Teslin and the Teslin Tlingit Council, politicians and civil servants from both sides recognized their institutional strengths and weaknesses and used that information to coordinate where costly duplication was a potential danger. Interviewees from both communities recognized that it did not make sense to build two indoor ice rinks or two skateboard parks, for instance, so they collaborated in ways that recognized the strengths that each government brought to the table. Identifying institutional differences and the ways in which they complement the strengths and weaknesses of the other government is one way to eliminate resources as a constraint and to foster collaborative willingness on both sides.

Similarly, Indigenous and local leaders might try to identify the different sets of imperatives that both communities have, paying particular attention to aligning convenient versus necessary imperatives. In the case of the Village of Haines Junction and the Champagne and Aishihik First Nations, there was willingness and capacity for fostering collaboration, but nothing highly intense emerged because each government had prioritized different goals for their communities. Being able to recognize one's own imperatives and the imperatives of a neighbouring government should help Indigenous and local leaders to find ways for creating partnerships along multiple issues that benefit both communities.

Finally, Indigenous and local policymakers might attempt to strengthen community capital. These activities might include hosting more community events aimed at both communities, creating opportunities for community leaders to make connections with their counterparts in hopes of generating champions for intergovernmental partnerships, and establishing personal relationships with their political counterparts in the other communities. Our findings suggest that the presence of strong community capital creates the necessary space for all other factors to line up to produce cooperation. A shared civic identity predisposes political leaders and civil servants to being open and welcoming of collaborative proposals from their Indigenous or local counterparts. Moreover, governments are not the only actors that can influence Indigenous–local intergovernmental relations. Citizens and community leaders can also engage in activities that encourage intergovernmental cooperation. By independently forging links with their Indigenous or local counterparts, they too can contribute to a stronger sense of shared civic identity. Without the presence of community capital, cooperation and communication are simply more difficult to achieve (Fraser and Viswanathan 2013; Wood 2003).

For the scholarly community, our research provides a useful framework for making sense of and doing further work on this important and emerging topic. Scholars can build on our work by applying our framework to comparative studies of Indigenous–local intergovernmental relations in the United States, Australia, and New Zealand (see Walker 2008, 22–3). Or they might use our typology and framework to look at other types of intergovernmental or multilevel governance partnerships. Others might take up the normative questions that are left unanswered in this study by examining more carefully how these relationships are benefiting (or not) their communities and whether these partnerships are different from those that exist at the federal, provincial, and territorial levels. Finally, some scholars might analyse the outcomes of these partnerships and find a way to measure their effectiveness at improving relationships or addressing internal or common problems (see Belanger and Walker 2009). We think this book has only scratched the surface of this important and emerging trend, and we hope that others will build on our work to examine the quiet evolution that is occurring at the Indigenous–local level in Canada.

References

Abele, F., and K. Graham. 1989. "High Politics Is Not Enough: Services for Aboriginal Peoples in Alberta and Ontario." In *Defining the Responsibilities: Federal and Provincial Governments and Aboriginal Peoples*, ed. D. Hawkes. Ottawa, Carleton University Press.

– 2011. "Federal Urban Aboriginal Policy: The Challenge of Viewing the Stars in the Urban Night Sky." In Peters 2011, 33–520.

Abele, F., R. Lapointe, D.J. Leech, and M. McCrossan. 2011. "Aboriginal People and Public Policy in Four Ontario Cities." In Peters 2011, 87–126.

Abele, F., and M.J. Prince. 2002. "Alternative Futures: Aboriginal Peoples and Canadian Federalism." In *Canadian Federalism: Performance, Effectiveness, and Legitimacy*, ed. H. Bakvis and G. Skogstad, 220–37. Oxford: Oxford University Press.

– 2003. "Aboriginal Governance and Canadian Federalism: A To-Do List for Canada." In *New Trends in Canadian Federalism*, ed. F. Rocher and M. Smith, 135–65. Toronto: Broadview.

Aboriginal Affairs and Northern Development Canada. 2013, 2014. Batchewana First Nation Detail. http://pse5-esd5.ainc-inac.gc.ca/fnp/Main/Search/FNMain.aspx?BAND_NUMBER=198&lang=eng.

– 2014. Première Nation Malécite de Viger. http://www.aadnc-aandc.gc.ca/Mobile/Nations/profile_viger-eng.html.

Across the River Consulting and Urban Systems. 2013. *Teslin Municipal Services Financial Analysis*. http://www.community.gov.yk.ca/community_affairs/pdf/Teslin_MSFA_Final_Report.pdf.

Alcantara, C. 2006. "Indian Women and the Division of Matrimonial Real Property on Canadian Indian Reserves." *Canadian Journal of Women and the Law* 18 (2): 513–33.

– 2010. "Indigenous Contentious Collective Action in Canada: The Labrador Innu and Their Occupation of the Goose Bay Military Air Base." *Canadian Journal of Native Studies* 30 (1): 21–43.

– 2013. *Negotiating the Deal: Comprehensive Land Claims Agreements in Canada*. Toronto: University of Toronto Press.

Alcantara, C., and J. Nelles. 2009. "Claiming the City: Co-operation and Making the Deal in Urban Comprehensive Land Claims Negotiations in Canada." *Canadian Journal of Political Science / Revue canadienne de science politique* 42 (3): 705–27. http://dx.doi.org/10.1017/S0008423909990394.

– 2014. "Indigenous Peoples and the State in Settler Societies: Toward a More Robust Definition of Multilevel Governance." *Publius* 44 (1): 183–204. http://dx.doi.org/10.1093/publius/pjt013.

Alcantara, C., and G. Whitfield. 2010. "Aboriginal Self-Government through Constitutional Design: A Survey of Fourteen Aboriginal Constitutions in Canada." *Journal of Canadian Studies / Revue d'études canadiennes* 44 (2): 122–45.

Alcantara, C., and G. Wilson. 2014. "The Dynamics of Intra-Jurisdictional Relations in the Inuit Regions of the Canadian Arctic: An Institutionalist Perspective." *Regional & Federal Studies* 24 (1): 43–61. http://dx.doi.org/10.1080/13597566.2013.818981.

Alfred, T. 1999. *Peace, Power, Righteousness*. Toronto: Oxford University Press.

Amaroso, D. 2013. Interview by Z. Spicer, 28 October.

Andersen, C., and J. Strachan. 2011. "Urban Aboriginal Programming in a Coordination Vacuum: The Alberta (Dis)Advantage." In Peters 2011, 127–59.

Apostle, N. 2013. Interview by Z. Spicer, 29 October.

Armour, K. 2014. Interview by Z. Spicer.

Assemblée Nationale. 2013. "Loi concernant la Municipalité régionale de comté des Basques." Project de loi no 206. Ville de Québec: Éditeur Officiel du Québec.

Bel, G., and M.E. Warner. 2015. "Inter-Municipal Cooperation and Costs: Expectations and Evidence." *Public Administration* 93 (1): 52–67. http://dx.doi.org/10.1111/padm.12104.

Belanger, Y.D., and W. Lackenbauer, eds. 2014. *Blockades or Breakthroughs? Aboriginal Peoples Confront the Canadian State*. Montreal and Kingston: McGill-Queen's University Press.

Belanger, Y.D., and R. Walker. 2009. "Interest Convergence and Co-Production of Plans: An Examination of Winnipeg's 'Aboriginal Pathways.'" *Canadian Journal of Urban Research* 18 (1): 118–39.

Birkland, T.A. 1997. *After Disaster: Agenda Setting, Public Policy, and Focusing Events*. Washington, DC: Georgetown University Press.

By-Law to Authorize the Entering into of an Agreement between the Pembroke Regional Hospital, City of Pembroke, Township of Laurentian Valley, Algonquins of Pikwakagan First Nation, Town of Petawawa, Township of Whitewater Region, Township of Bonnechere Valley and North Algona Wilberforce Township to Formally Establish "The Upper Ottawa Valley Medical Recruitment Committee." 2011.

Calderhead, C., and J.-L. Klein. 2012. "L'identité et le territoire dans la reconstruction communautaire des Malécites de Viger." *Cahiers de géographie de Québec* 56 (159): 583–98. http://dx.doi.org/10.7202/1015308ar.

Calderhead, M. 2011. "La reconstruction identitaire et territoriale d'une communauté dispersée: L'ere de restitution pour les Malecites de Viger?" Master's thesis, Université de Québec.

Champagne and Aishihik First Nations. 1993a. "The Champagne and Aishihik First Nations Final Agreement."

– 1993b. "The Champagne and Aishihik First Nations Self-Government Agreement."

– 2007. *Champagne and Aishihik First Nations 2006–2007 Annual Report.*

– 2012. "Constitution of the Champagne and Aishihik First Nations."

– 2014. "Integrated Community Sustainability Plan." Draft.

Chez les Basques. 2014. L'histoire. http://www.tourismelesbasques.com/fr/chez-les-basques/l-histoire.

City of Kamloops and Kamloops Indian Band. 2008. "Fire Protection Agreement."

City of Prince Albert and Saskatchewan First Nations and Metis Relations. 2008. "Employer Partnership Agreement between the City of Prince Albert and Saskatchewan First Nations and Metis Relations. Saskatoon, SK.

Coates, K., and W.R. Morrison. 2009. "From Panacea to Reality: The Practicalities of Canadian Aboriginal Self-Government Agreements." In *Aboriginal Self-Government in Canada*, ed. Y.D. Belanger, 105–22. Saskatoon: Purich.

Coleman, J.S. 1988. "Social Capital in the Creation of Human Capital." In "Sociological Analysis of Economic Institutions," supplement, *American Journal of Sociology* 94:S95–S120. http://dx.doi.org/10.1086/228943.

Conseil de la Première Nation Malécite de Viger et La Municipalité Régionale de Comté des Basques. 2014. "Entente Particulière sur la Gestion et la Mise en Valeur du Parc Régional Inter-Nations."

Corbiere, J. 2013. Interview by C. Alcantara, 28 October.

Coulthard, G.S., and T. Alfred. 2014. *Red Skins, White Masks: Rejecting the Colonial Politics of Recognition*. Minneapolis: University of Minnesota Press. http://dx.doi.org/10.5749/minnesota/9780816679645.001.0001.

Crawshay, M. 2014. Interview by C. Alcantara, 28 July.

Curran, G. 2014. Interview by Z. Spicer, 9 April.

Curry, D. 2004. *Debwewin: A Three-City Anti-Racism Initiative in Northeastern Ontario Sault Ste Marie Report*. http://www.debwewin.ca/northbayreport.pdf.

Dallaire, C. 2014. *Activity Report*. http://textlab.io/doc/405340/volume-6-number-1-march-2014---premi%C3%A8re-nation-mal%C3%A9cite-d.

Della-Mattia, E. 2009. "New Ambulance Base to Open in Garden River." *Sault Star*, 24 November.

Denis, B. 2014. Interview by X. Beriault, October.

Dickason, O.P., and W. Newbigging. 2010. *A Concise History of Canada's First Nations*. Toronto: Oxford University Press.

Ditidaht First Nation and Town of Ladysmith. 1999. "Proposed Partnership between the Ditidaht First Nation and Ladysmith: Developing Capacity for Self-Government." Town of Ladysmith, BC.

Evans, L.E. 2011. "Expertise and Scale of Conflict: Governments as Advocates in American Indian Politics." *American Political Science Review* 105 (4): 663–82. http://dx.doi.org/10.1017/S0003055411000347.

Evers, A. 2003. "Social Capital and Civic Commitment: On Putnam's Way of Understanding." *Social Policy and Society* 2 (1): 13–21. http://dx.doi.org/10.1017/S1474746403001052.

Fata, F. 2013. Interview by Z. Spicer, 28 October.

Federation of Canadian Municipalities. 2011. *First Nations–Municipal Community Infrastructure Partnership Program: Service Agreement Toolkit*. http://www.fcm.ca/Documents/tools/CIPP/CIPP_Toolkit_EN.pdf.

Feiock, R.C. 2008. "Metropolitan Governance and Institutional Collective Action." *Urban Affairs Review* 44 (3): 356–77. http://dx.doi.org/10.1177/1078087408324000.

Flanagan, T. 2008. *First Nations? Second Thoughts*. Montreal and Kingston: McGill-Queen's University Press.

Fraser, C.M., and L. Viswanathan. 2013. "The Crown Duty to Consult and Ontario Municipal–First Nations Relations: Lessons Learned from the Red Hill Valley Parkway Project." *Canadian Journal of Urban Research* 22 (1): 1–19.

Fratesi, J. 2010. Interview by C. Alcantara, 23 August.

– 2013. Interview by C. Alcantara, 7 November.

Garden River First Nation. 2013. *Ketegaunseebee Garden River First Nation Community Plan*. ON: Garden River First Nation.

Gayda, M. 2012. "The Pipe at the Post: An Examination of Municipal–First Nation Intergovernmental Agreements in Canada." Master's thesis, Wilfrid Laurier University.

Gervais, K. 2014. Interview by C. Alcantara, 24 July.

Gillmore, M. 2012. "Trash Tops in Teslin Mayoral Race. *Yukon News*, 12 October.

Government of British Columbia. 2006. *Study Supports Local Government, First Nations.* http://www.gov.yk.ca/news/11-055.html.

Government of Yukon. 2011. "Yukon Highlights Emergency Preparedness Week with Operation Wildfire," news release, 5 May.

Greater Vancouver Regional District. 2005. *Aboriginal Affairs Update.*

Greitens, T.J., J.C. Strachan, and C. Welton. 2013. "The Importance of Multilevel Governance Participation in the 'Great Lakes Areas of Concern.'" In *Making Multilevel Public Management Work: Stories of Success and Failure from Europe and North America*, ed. D. Cepiku, D.K. Jesuit, and I. Roberge, 159–82. Boca Raton: CRC. http://dx.doi.org/10.1201/b14752-12.

Habitat for Humanity Yukon. 2012. "Champagne and Aishihik First Nations and Habitat for Humanity Yukon form Partnership," news release, 19 April.

Haudenosaunee Wildlife and Habitat Authority and Hamilton Conservation Authority. 2011. "Protocol between the Haudenosaunee Wildlife Conservation Authority and the Hamilton Conservation Authority."

Hawkins, C.V., and J.B. Carr. 2015. "The Costs of Services Cooperation: A Review of the Literature." In *Municipal Shared Services Consolidation: A Public Solutions Handbook*, ed. A. Henderson, 224–39. New York: Routledge.

Hedican, E.J. 2013. *Ipperwash: The Tragic Failure of Canada's Aboriginal Policy.* Toronto: University of Toronto Press.

Henderson, A. 2008. "Self-Government in Nunavut." In *Aboriginal Self-Government in Canada: Current Trends and Issues*, ed. Y.D. Belanger, 222–39. Saskatoon: Purich Publishing.

Henton, D., and J.G. Melville. 1997. *Grassroots Leaders for a New Economy: How Civic Entrepreneurs Are Building Prosperous Communities.* New York: Jossey-Bass.

Hodgson, G.M. 2006. "What Are Institutions?" *Journal of Economic Issues* 40 (1): 1–25. http://dx.doi.org/10.1080/00213624.2006.11506879.

Howitt, R., K. Doohan, S. Suchet-Pearson, and S. Cross. 2013. "Capacity Deficits at Cultural Interfaces of Land and Sea Governance." In *Reclaiming Indigenous Planning*, ed. R. Walker, T. Jojola, and D. Natcher, 313–38. Montreal and Kingston: McGill-Queen's University Press.

Hulst, R., and A. van Montfort. 2007. "Inter-Municipal Cooperation: A Widespread Phenomenon." In *Inter-Municipal Cooperation in Europe*, ed. R. Hulst and A. van Montfort, 1–21. Dordrecht: Springer. http://dx.doi.org/10.1007/1-4020-5379-7_1.

Huot, L.-P. 1999. Opinion du Juge Letarte, Cour d'Appel Province de Quebec, 200-09-002219-985, 15 June.

Irlbacher-Fox, S. 2010. *Finding Dahshaa: Self-Government, Social Suffering and Aboriginal Policy in Canada*. Vancouver: University of British Columbia Press.

Journal des débats de la Commission de l'aménagement du territoire. 2012. Entendre les intéressés et procéder à l'étude détaillée du projet de loi d'intérêt privé n° 206, Loi concernant la Municipalité régionale de comté des Basques. http://www.assnat.qc.ca/fr/travaux-parlementaires/commissions/cat-40-1/journal-debats/CAT-130611-5.html.

Kelly, B. 2013. "No Joke: Transit Says No." *Sault Star*, 7 April.

Kino-nda-niimi Collective. 2013. *The Winter We Danced: Voices from the Past, Future and the Idle No More Movement*. Winnipeg: ARP Books.

Ktunaxa Nation, Regional District of East Kootenay, Regional District of Central Kootenay, City of Cranbrook, City of Kimberley, City of Fernie, ... Village of Canal Flats. 2005. "Memorandum of Understanding – Issue: Communication." Regional District of East Kootenay, BC.

Kulchyski, P. 2013. *Aboriginal Rights Are Not Human Rights: In Defence of Aboriginal Struggles*. Winnipeg: ARP Books.

Kwon, S.-W., and R.C. Feiock. 2010. "Overcoming the Barriers to Cooperation: Intergovernmental Service Agreements." *Public Administration Review* 70 (6): 876–84. http://dx.doi.org/10.1111/j.1540-6210.2010.02219.x.

Larouche, A. 2014. Interview by X. Beriault, October.

Lin, N. 2001. *Social Capital: A Theory of Social Structure and Action*. Cambridge: Cambridge University Press. http://dx.doi.org/10.1017/CBO9780511815447.

McConnell, D. 2013. Interview by Z. Spicer, 30 October.

Miller, J.R. 2000. *Skyscrapers Hide the Heavens: A History of Indian-White Relations in Canada*. Toronto: University of Toronto Press.

– 2009. *Compact, Contract, Covenant: Aboriginal Treaty-Making in Canada*. Toronto: University of Toronto Press.

Ministère d'affaires municipales et Occupation du Territoire Québec. 2010. Répertoire des municipalités: Les Basques. http://www.mamrot.gouv.qc.ca/repertoire-des-municipalites/fiche/mrc/110/.

– 2014. *L'organisation municipale et régionale au Québec en 2014*. http://www.mamrot.gouv.qc.ca/pub/organisation_municipale/organisation_territoriale/organisation_municipale.pdf.

Ministère d'immigration diversité et inclusion Québec. 2014. Bas-Saint-Laurent. http://www.immigration-quebec.gouv.qc.ca/en/settle/bas-saint-laurent.html.

Moore, J., R. Walker, and I. Skelton. 2011. "Challenging the New Canadian Myth: Colonialism, Post-Colonialism and Urban Aboriginal Policy in Thompson and Brandon, Manitoba." *Canadian Journal of Native Studies* 31 (1): 17–42.

Morden, M. 2013. "Telling Stories about Conflict: Symbolic Politics and the Ipperwash Land Transfer Agreement." *Canadian Journal of Political Science / Revue canadienne de science politique* 46 (3): 505–24. http://dx.doi.org/10.1017/S0008423913000668.

Municipal–Aboriginal Adjacent Community Cooperation Project. 2002. *Partnerships in Practice: Case Studies in Municipal and First Nations' Economic Development Co-operation.* http://www.ubcm.ca/assets/library/Policy~Topics/First~Nations~Relations/Relationship~Building~and~Dispute~Resolution~Resources/Partnerships%20in%20Practice%202002.pdf.

Murray, K.B. 2011. "The Silence of Urban Aboriginal Policy in New Brunswick." In Peters 2011, 53–86.

Nadasdy, Paul. 2003. *Hunters and Bureaucrats: Power, Knowledge, and Aboriginal-State Relations in the Southwest Yukon.* Vancouver: UBC Press.

Nadeau, M. 2013. Interview by Z. Spicer, 31 October.

Nelles, J. 2012. *Comparative Metropolitan Politics: Governing beyond Local Boundaries and the Imagined Metropolis.* London: Routledge.

Nelles, J., and C. Alcantara. 2011. "Strengthening the Ties That Bind? An Analysis of Aboriginal–Municipal Intergovernmental Agreements in British Columbia." *Canadian Public Administration* 54 (3): 315–34. http://dx.doi.org/10.1111/j.1754-7121.2011.00178.x.

– 2014. "Explaining the Emergence of Indigenous–Local Intergovernmental Relations in Settler Societies: A Theoretical Framework." *Urban Affairs Review* 50 (5): 599–622. http://dx.doi.org/10.1177/1078087413501638.

North, D. 1990. *Institutions, Institutional Change and Economic Performance.* Cambridge: Cambridge University Press. http://dx.doi.org/10.1017/CBO9780511808678.

Olson, M. 1965. *The Logic of Collective Action.* Cambridge, MA: Harvard University Press.

Ontario Ministry of Municipal Affairs and Housing. 2009. *Municipal–Aboriginal Relationships: Case Studies.* Toronto: Queen's Printer.

Papillon, M. 2008. "Canadian Federalism and the Emerging Mosaic of Aboriginal Multilevel Governance." In *Canadian Federalism: Performance, Effectiveness, and Legitimacy,* ed. H. Bakvis and G. Skogstad, 291–313. Toronto: Oxford University Press Canada.

Paquette, J., and G. Fallon. 2010. *First Nations Education Policy in Canada: Progress or Gridlock?* Toronto: University of Toronto Press.

Peters, E.J., ed. 2011. *Urban Aboriginal Policy Making in Canadian Municipalities.* Montreal and Kingston: McGill-Queen's University Press.

Poelzer, G., and K. Coates. 2015. *From Treaty Peoples to Treaty Nation.* Vancouver: UBC Press.

Potapchuk, W.R., and J.P. Crocker Jr. 1999. "Exploring the Elements of Civic Capital." *National Civic Review* 88 (3): 175–202. http://dx.doi.org/10.1002/ncr.88303.

Première Nation Malécite de Viger et MRC les Basques. 2013a. "Développement Économique." http://vigermalecite.com/services/developpement-economique/.

– 2013b. Trois-Pistoles, QC: Le Territoire Public de la Région des Basques.

– 2013c. "Two Nations, One Celebration."

Przeworski, A., and H. Teune. 1970. *The Logic of Comparative Social Inquiry.* New York: Wiley-Interscience.

Purvis, M. 2008. "Did You Know 40 First Nations in Ontario Have No Fire Service?" *Sault Star*, 28 June.

Putnam, R.D. 2000. *Bowling Alone: The Collapse and Revival of American Community.* New York: Simon & Schuster. http://dx.doi.org/10.1145/358916.361990.

Radio-Canada. 2013, 15 January. "Le gardien du club de chasse privé Appalaches en procès." http://www.radio-canada.ca/regions/est-quebec/2013/01/15/008-basques-proces-gardien-club-appalaches.shtml.

Riseborough, M. 2012. Email correspondence, 26 January.

– 2014. Interview by C. Alcantara, 28 July.

Royal Commission on Aboriginal Peoples (RCAP). 1996. *Report of the Royal Commission on Aboriginal Peoples.* Ottawa: Aboriginal Affairs and Northern Canada. http://www.lop.parl.gc.ca/content/lop/researchpublications/prb9924-e.htm.

Rufiange-Holway, T. 2014. Interview by Z. Spicer, 7 August.

Ruru, J. 2008. "Recent Legislation Comment: Finding Solutions for the Legislative Gaps in Determining Rights to the Family Home on Colonially Defined Indigenous Lands." *University of British Columbia Law Review* 41 (2): 315–48.

Sanquer, S. 2014. Interview by X. Bériault, 21 October.

Sayers, L. 2013. Interview by Z. Spicer, 30 October.

Sayers, P. 2013. Interview by Z. Spicer, 29 October.

Scott, D. 2013. Interview by Z. Spicer, 29 October.

Smith, C. 2014. Interview by Z. Spicer, 12 April.

Spicer, Z. 2014. "The Ties That Bind? Exploring the Dynamics of Inter-Municipal Agreement Formation between Separated Cities and Counties." *Canadian Public Policy* 40 (3): 245–58. http://dx.doi.org/10.3138/cpp.2013-051.

Statistics Canada. 2011a. "National Household Survey."

– 2011b. "Population, Urban and Rural, by Province and Territory."

– 2012. "Teslin, Yukon and Yukon, Yukon (table) Census Profiles."

Tamera Services Ltd. 2002. *Report Governing Relations between Local Government and First Nation Government.* www.cd.govbc.ca/lgd/gov_structure/library/first_nations_report.pdf.

Taylor, D. 2013. "Chief Sayers Still Hopes for Bus Route." *Sault Star*, 21 April.

Taylor, K. 2014. Interview by Z. Spicer, 10 April.

Teslin Tlingit Council. 1993a. "The Teslin Tlingit Council Final Agreement."

– 1993b. "The Teslin Tlingit Council Self-Government Agreement."

– 2013. "Teslin Tlingit Council Constitution."

– 2014a. *Deslin Neek: The Voice of the Teslin Tlingit Council* (March/April).

– 2014b. Homepage. http://www.ttc-teslin.com/our-people.html.

Tully, Jim. 2001. *Reconsidering the BC Treaty Process.* Ottawa: Law Commission of Canada.

Union of British Columbia Municipalities. 2000. "Land Use Coordination, Servicing and Dispute Resolution: Towards Certainty for Local Government through Treaty Negotiations." http://www.ubcm.ca/assets/Resolutions~and~Policy/Policy~Papers/2000/Land%20Use%20Coordination%20Servicing%20and%20Dispute%20Resolution%202000.pdf.

Village of Haines Junction. 2014. Regular Council Meeting #13–14 Minutes.

Village of Haines Junction and Champagne and Aishihik First Nations. 2014. "Memorandum of Understanding between the Village of Haines Junction and the Champagne and Aishihik First Nations."

Village of Teslin. 2014. Homepage. http://www.teslin.ca/.

Village of Teslin and Teslin Tlingit Council. 2005a. "Infrastructure and Services Memorandum of Understanding."

– 2005b. "Skateboard Park Agreement."

– 2005c. "Teslin Sewer Development Agreement."

– 2009. "Our Towns, Our Future: Teslin Integrated Community Sustainability Plan."

– 2011. "Community of Teslin Recreation Contribution Agreement."

Wagner, W.E. 2004. "Beyond Dollars and Cents: Using Civic Capital to Fashion Urban Improvements." *City & Community* 3 (2): 157–73. http://dx.doi.org/10.1111/j.1535-6841.2004.00074.x.

Walker, R. 2008. "Improving the Interface between Urban Municipalities and Aboriginal Communities." In supplement, *Canadian Journal of Urban Research* 17 (1): S20–S36.

Walker, R., J. Moore, and M. Linklater. 2011. "More Than Stakeholders, Voices, and Tables: Towards Co-Production of Urban Aboriginal Policy in Manitoba." In Peters 2011, 160–201.

Westbank First Nation and Regional District of Central Okanagan. 1999. "Statement of Political Relationship between the Westbank First Nation and the Regional District of Central Okanagan January 1999." Regional District of Central Okanagan, BC.

White, G. 2009. "Governance in Nunavut: Capacity vs Culture?" *Journal of Canadian Studies* 43:57–81.

White, J.P., P. Maxim, and D.N. Beavon, eds. 2003. *Aboriginal Conditions: Research as a Foundation for Public Policy.* Vancouver: UBC Press.

Widdowson, F., and A. Howard. 2008. *Disrobing the Aboriginal Industry.* Montreal and Kingston: McGill-Queen's University Press.

Wilson, G.N. 2008. "Nested Federalism in Arctic Quebec: A Comparative Perspective." *Canadian Journal of Political Science / Revue canadienne de science politique* 41(1): 71–92.

Wirth, W. 2014. Interview by Z. Spicer, 9 April.

Wolfe, D.A., and J. Nelles. 2008. "The Role of Civic Capital and Civic Associations in Cluster Policy." In *Handbook of Research on Innovation and Clusters*, ed. C. Karlsson, 374–92. Cheltenham: Edward Elgar. http://dx.doi.org/10.4337/9781848445079.00030.

Wood, P. 2003. "A Road Runs through It: Aboriginal Citizenship at the Edge of Urban Development." *Citizenship Studies* 7 (4): 463–73. http://dx.doi.org/10.1080/1362102032000134985.

Wotherspoon, T., and J. Hansen. 2013. "The 'Idle No More' Movement: Paradoxes of First Nations Inclusion in the Canadian Context." *Social Inclusion* 1 (1): 21–36. http://dx.doi.org/10.17645/si.v1i1.107.

Wright, S. 2014. Interview by C. Alcantara, 28 July.

Zeemering, E.S. 2008. "Governing Interlocal Cooperation: City Council Interests and the Implications for Public Management." *Public Administration Review* 68 (4): 731–41. http://dx.doi.org/10.1111/j.1540-6210.2008.00911.x.

Index